DERBY COUNTY
IN FOCUS
1950-1970

ANDY ELLIS

DERBY COUNTY IN FOCUS
1950-1970

ANDY ELLIS

First published 2019 by DB Publishing, an imprint of JMD Media Ltd,
Nottingham, United Kingdom.

ISBN 978-1-78091-593-7

Printed in the UK

CONTENTS

Introduction

Raymonds Press Agency was built up by Klaus Jacoby, John Twells and Neil Hallam and was, at one point, the largest regional news agency in the country. At its peak it had offices in Chesterfield, Nottingham, Lincoln, Stoke, Ipswich, Norwich and its head office in Derby. It began in the 1930s and was eventually acquired by the free newspaper publisher and Derby County owner Lionel Pickering.

Raymonds Photographers (later Raymonds Press Agency) had been taking photographs of Derby County from the mid-1950s onwards, including many of the iconic matches, events, players and personalities that have graced the Baseball Ground and Pride Park during that time.

In this edition we will look back at some of the thousands of images captured of Derby County's home matches from the mid-1950s, when Raymonds first started covering the games, through to the start of the 1970s when the team were battling at the top of the First Division, breaking attendance records and rarely out of the newspaper headlines, thanks in part to the manager Brian Clough.

As Derby's name became stronger, demand for these images from the local press agency increased and many of them were sold around the world as well as newspapers and football magazines in the UK.

During the 20 years that this book covers, camera technology also progressed dramatically. The images from the 1950s are on glass plates and there followed various sizes of negatives until the popular 35mm size became the standard for photographers. Since then colour pictures have arisen and the press photographers are now equipped with laptops and digital cameras and thousands of pounds' worth of camera lenses, allowing them to take many more images at much better quality anywhere on the field, which can be sent around the world in seconds.

Long gone are the days of the photographer lying alongside the goals at the Baseball Ground on a groundsheet having to stop and change a reel of film and having despatch riders waiting to whisk them away to newspaper offices for printing. Lighting at stadia has improved dramatically as well, with Derby having very basic floodlights installed in the 1950s, but the strength of those lights combined with the relatively low-quality film and cameras meant night-time fixtures were very dark and grainy when produced as prints.

The cameras were very basic compared to the technology-driven marvels of today and the photographer had to be skilled to press the shutter button at just the right moment or anticipate when a shot, save or goal might happen, before the opportunity passed. The modern cameras will have a 'burst mode' capability that allows lots of images to be captured in a short space of time, where the best image can be selected and the rest disregarded.

With computer-based storing of images, the old method of glass plates, negatives and prints has ceased and these original items, with or without copyright, are increasingly sought after and prices are on the up.

With Raymonds going out of business in 2010, the liquidators sold the back catalogue of football negatives, together with the copyright to them, allowing publications like this to come about.

Images are mixed with programmes and other items of memorabilia. Crowd scenes also reveal changes in society … war dress, hats, women …

If you want to purchase prints of the images contained in this book, then contact should be made directly with the author at andy.ellis@eighteen84. co.uk.

Andy Ellis
September 2019

1950s

The immediate years after the FA Cup win in 1946 saw a boom in attendances and saw Derby finish in fourth and third places in successive years. This was aided by them breaking the British transfer record twice in two years, firstly by signing Billy Steel for £15,500 and then paying £24,500 for Manchester United forward Johnny Morris.

Steel left after three seasons and Morris left after five games of the 1952-53 season, which saw them relegated to the Second Division and a parting of the ways with the cup-winning manager Stuart McMillan.

Former player Jack Barker had taken over as manager and, for the first time since 1926, Derby kicked off in Division Two. Performances did not improve, with an 18th-place finish, just four points away from relegation. That relegation

1950-51. The squad that the began the decade in the First Division and just four years after lifting the FA Cup. Back: Poole (trainer), Cushlow, Mozley, Brown, Townsend, Oliver, Parr, Musson, Mays, Bowers (assistant trainer). Middle: Bell, McLaren, Stamps, McMillan (manager), Lee, Morris, Powell, Parry, Mynard. Front: Ward, Parkin, Harrison, Walker, McLachlan, Wilkins.

Johnny Morris was signed from Manchester United in March 1949 by paying a British record fee of £24,500. He scored 13 goals in his first 13 games that earnt him an England call up. After three years, in which he scored 47 goals in 140 games, he moved to Leicester City.

was only temporarily postponed despite a flurry of transfer activity towards the end of the season, when it was too late to have any effect. So, in less than nine years they had gone from winning the FA Cup and being rated as one of the best and most attractive teams to watch in the country to being a Third Division outfit.

Another former player, Harry Storer, had been installed as manager by August 1955 and his new squad of players had Derby finishing in second place, which was not good enough to get promotion as the Third Division was regionalised into North and South sections and only the top team in each section would get promotion. No mistake was made the following year, with the team being promoted by winning the league in fine style by four clear points and scoring a club record of 111 goals, with Ray Straw equalling the club record of 37 goals, set some years previously by Jack Bowers.

For all this league success, the FA Cup competition turned out to be an embarrassment, with non-league opposition knocking them out in the early stages in two successive seasons. After squeezing past Crook Town after a replay, Boston United came to the Baseball Ground with half a team of former Derby players and won 6-1, which is still one of the biggest shocks ever in the competition, and again the following year New Brighton won 3-1 at the Baseball Ground.

Following their promotion back into Division Two, Derby struggled to make an impression in the league, but were stable enough to become an established team. It was a hard-working, physical team that Storer had built but there was never enough money to attract good-quality players to come into the club and

make the progress required to challenge for a promotion place. A seventh place in 1958-59 was to be the highest finishing position since the relegation from Division One. 1959-60 brought the thoughts of relegation back into the minds of the Rams fans as some poor performances had them in constant trouble.

Billy Steel's £15,500 transfer from Morton to Derby County in 1947 was a British record for one of Scotland's greatest inside-forwards. Steel was not always popular at the Baseball Ground, especially among his fellow professionals. After three years he returned to Scotland when Dundee paid a Scottish record fee of £22,500.

3e jaargang No. 7 — 23 Mei 1951

HET STADION NIEUWS

STADION

„FEIJENOORD"

Neêrlands grootste sportcentrum

The end-of-season tour in 1951 went to Holland and took in four games in seven days, the first playing against the Dutch B team at the Feyenoord stadium in Rotterdam, which the home side won 5-3. This was followed by a game against a Dutch XI and Bondesftal (both in Utrecht) and Netherlands in Amsterdam.

A 1952 team that saw Johnny Morris leaving just five games into the 1952-53 season. Back: J. Morris, H. Lee, T. Powell, R. Middleton, K. Oliver, W. Musson. Front: R. Harrison, J. Parry, J. Stamps, A. Mays, B. Mozley.

Derby's first floodlit match at the Baseball Ground was against Notts County on 16 March 1953 and the programme has a special cover that was to be used for many floodlit matches during the next couple of seasons. The lights initially consisted of 15 lamps on a crude scaffold frame and there were four of these structures positioned on the corners of the Osmaston and Normanton stands. These were to remain in use, although increased to 25 lamps per frame, until the 1970s.

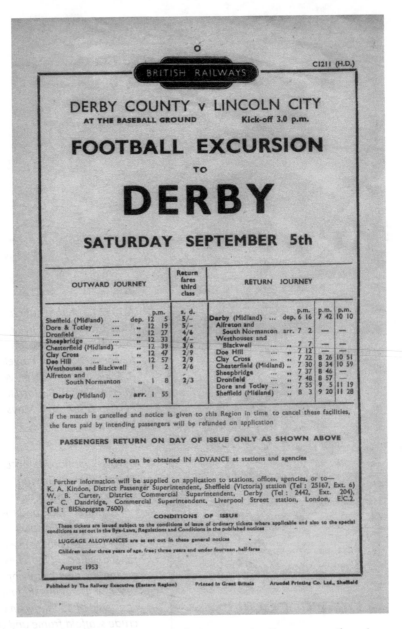

BRITISH RAILWAYS

C1211 (H.D.)

DERBY COUNTY v LINCOLN CITY

AT THE BASEBALL GROUND   **Kick-off 3.0 p.m.**

FOOTBALL EXCURSION

TO

DERBY

SATURDAY SEPTEMBER 5th

OUTWARD JOURNEY			Return fares third class	RETURN JOURNEY				
		p.m.	s. d.			p.m.	p.m.	p.m.
Sheffield (Midland) ...	dep.	12 5	5/-	Derby (Midland) ...	dep. 6 16		7 42	10 10
Dore & Totley ...	„	12 19	5/-	Alfreton and				
Dronfield	„	12 27	4/6	South Normanton arr. 7 2		—	—	
Sheepbridge ...	„	12 33	4/-	Westhouses and				
Chesterfield (Midland)	„	12 39	3/6	Blackwell ...	„ 7 7	—	—	
Clay Cross	„	12 47	2/9	Doe Hill	„ 7 12	—	—	
Doe Hill	„	12 57	2/9	Clay Cross ...	„ 7 22	8 26	10 51	
Westhouses and Blackwell	„	1 2	2/6	Chesterfield (Midland)	„ 7 30	8 34	10 59	
Alfreton and				Sheepbridge ...	„ 7 37	8 46	—	
South Normanton	„	1 8	2/3	Dronfield ...	„ 7 48	8 57	—	
				Dore and Totley ...	„ 7 55	9 5	11 19	
Derby (Midland) ...	arr.	1 55		Sheffield (Midland)	„ 8 3	9 20	11 28	

If the match is cancelled and notice is given to this Region in time to cancel these facilities, the fares paid by intending passengers will be refunded on application

PASSENGERS RETURN ON DAY OF ISSUE ONLY AS SHOWN ABOVE

Tickets can be obtained IN ADVANCE at stations and agencies

Further information will be supplied on application to stations, offices, agencies, or to— K. A. Kindon, District Passenger Superintendent, Sheffield (Victoria) station (Tel : 25167, Ext. 6) W. B. Carter, District Commercial Superintendent, Derby (Tel : 2442, Ext. 204), or C. Dandridge, Commercial Superintendent, Liverpool Street station, London, E.C.2. (Tel : BIShopsgate 7600)

CONDITIONS OF ISSUE

These tickets are issued subject to the conditions of issue of ordinary tickets where applicable and also to the special conditions as set out in the Bye-Laws, Regulations and Conditions in the published notices

LUGGAGE ALLOWANCES are as set out in these general notices

Children under three years of age, free; three years and under fourteen, half-fares

August 1953

Published by The Railway Executive (Eastern Region)   Printed in Great Britain   Arundel Printing Co. Ltd., Sheffield

With no motorways and far fewer cars being owned, railways were the primary means of public transport between cities. 'Football Special' trains were often run on a Saturday to carry supporters from outlying towns and cities into Derby for the match and also take Derby supporters to the away matches.

The example bill is for the match against Lincoln City at the Baseball Ground on 5 September 1953 and it started in Sheffield at 12:05pm and arrived in Derby at 13:55pm. The cost for a return ticket was 5 shillings (25p).

This was the 1954-55 squad that was to see Derby relegated to the third tier of football for the first time in their history. This was taken in the gym at the Baseball Ground and includes Reg Harrison, Bert Mozley, Jack Parry, Geoff Barrowcliffe and Tommy Powell.

13 September 1954: this team lost 2-5 in an away match against Blackburn Rovers in the season that saw them finish bottom of Division Two. This defeat left them in 19th place. Derby's goals came from Powell and Dunn. Back: Parry, Mozley, Hunter, Upton, Bell, Davies. Front: Savin, Powell, Barrowcliffe, Dunn, McQuillan.

20 November 1954 v Rotherham United. The crowd at the Osmaston End shows very few women and children, no scarves and many men in similar overcoats and wearing a shirt and tie. Unfortunately, they saw yet another home defeat, 2-3, leaving them in 21st place.

December 1954. With the Baseball Ground pitch either muddy, flooded or frozen during the winter months, the nearest place to have a kickabout or do some basic training was on the car park of the adjacent Baseball Hotel.

The Christmas of 1954 saw the end of war-time rationing and the pantomime at the Hippodrome was 'Babes in the Wood' starring Stan Stennett together with a young duo, Morecambe and Wise. The picture show actress Gladys Joyce giving players a tour of the stage set.

Geoff Barrowcliffe was born in Little Eaton and Derby County was his only professional club, joining from Ilkeston Town in October 1950. Over the course of 14 years he played 503 games and scored 39 goals.

A snow-covered Baseball Ground in January 1955 looking from the Osmaston End terracing across to the Popside terracing.

With the game postponed, players posed for the cameras having a kickabout with a football-sized snowball at the Osmaston End.

A remaining thin layer of snow covered a frozen pitch, making for difficult conditions against Bristol Rovers on 19 February 1955. A Tommy Powell goal was equalised as Terry Webster (capped) can only watch on. Derby were not to win a game until the last match of the season.

Birmingham City, March 1955. A Birmingham attack is stopped. The initial set of floodlights can be seen in the distance. The number of lights would be increased as more floodlit games took place.

The last game of the 1954-55 season was a home game against Hull City and we can see goal-mouth action as Parry threatens to score. Derby won 3-0 but finished in last place and were relegated to the third tier of football for the first time in their history.

Harry Storer had been a Derby player back in the mid-1920s and made 274 appearances. He also played cricket for Derbyshire on 302 occasions. He was appointed manager in June 1955 as Derby embarked on their first season in Division Three (North).

Irishman Reg Ryan was Harry Storer's first signing in 1955 for £3,000 from West Bromwich Albion as Derby faced life in the Third Division for the first time. He won one cap for the Republic of Ireland and was a major force in getting Derby back into Division Two within two years, after 139 appearances and 31 goals.

Derby's first game at this level was on Saturday, 20 August 1955, with an unusual 6:45pm kick-off. A comfortable 4-0 win followed with goals from Ackerman, Mays and Pye. Here is Jack Parry (right) watching another chance go by with Tommy Powell and Reg Harrison in the distance.

The game against Workington in October 1955 was the first competitive one between the clubs and ended in a 2-2 draw, with Jack Parry and Tommy Powell scoring for The Rams.

Derby County Football Club Ltd.

Baseball Ground - Derby

Monday, 7th November, 1955

KICK-OFF 7.15 p.m.

DERBY COUNTY

versus

ALL STARS XI

Official Programme

3ᵈ.

Printed by Derwent Press Ltd. Derby, for Friary Publicity Ltd. Derby.

This fixture against an All Star XI was a benefit game for Walter 'Chick' Musson's family in November 1955. A tough-tackling left-back, he was another locally born player and was part of the 1946 FA Cup-winning team. He was diagnosed with leukaemia in June 1954 and died ten months later aged 34.

The Boy's Pen at the Baseball Ground being encouraged by a cheerleader dressed in black and white, ringing a bell. The view from here was never good being low down and in the corner, but it never worried the kids paying 9d (4p) to get in and hopping over the fence to the Normanton terrace. A disabled section is nearby where you can see some old motorised wheelchairs.

Being in the Third Division meant an early entry into the FA Cup and Derby were drawn away to Crook Town in the first round. The game that was played on 19 November 1955 ended in a 2-2 draw. The programme from this game is now very rare.

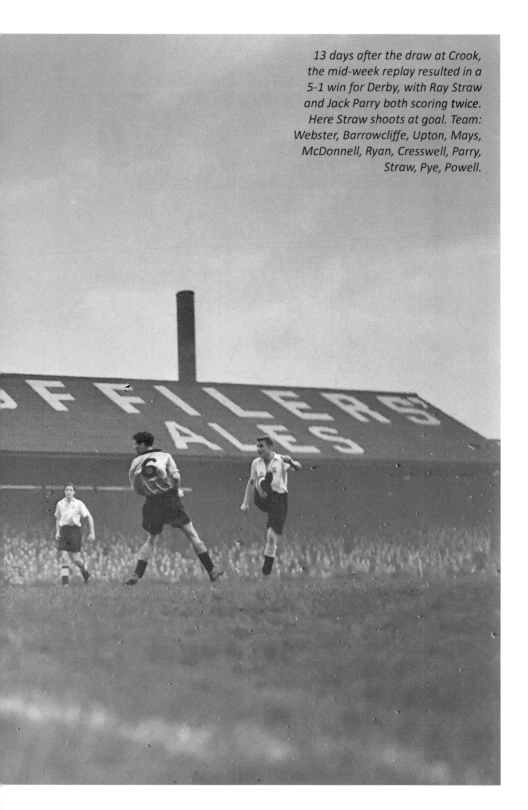

13 days after the draw at Crook, the mid-week replay resulted in a 5-1 win for Derby, with Ray Straw and Jack Parry both scoring twice. Here Straw shoots at goal. Team: Webster, Barrowcliffe, Upton, Mays, McDonnell, Ryan, Cresswell, Parry, Straw, Pye, Powell.

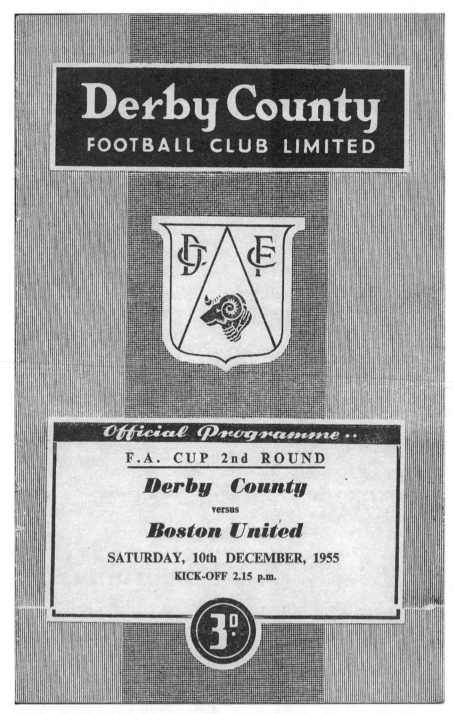

Derby County
FOOTBALL CLUB LIMITED

Official Programme..

F.A. CUP 2nd ROUND

Derby County

versus

Boston United

SATURDAY, 10th DECEMBER, 1955

KICK-OFF 2.15 p.m.

3^D

The FA Cup second round brought another non-league opponent, this time Boston United. The Boston team had six former Derby players in their team and pulled off one of the shock results in the competition's history, an astonishing 6-1 win.

Dennis Woodhead signs for Derby from Chesterfield for £1,500 after playing at Saltergate for just four months after his transfer from Sheffield Wednesday.

Roy Martin is welcomed at Derby railway station by some of his new teammates following his transfer from Birmingham City at the beginning of March 1956. The full-back went on to play 85 games over the next four years.

BARROW A.F.C. LTD.

Official Programme - Price 1d.

Saturday, 17th March, 1956

DERBY COUNTY

KICK-OFF 3-0 p.m.

by " CLUBMAN "

THE task of writing these notes is one of the most difficult I have had for a long time. Just what can one say after last week's " performance " at Oldham ? Let us be perfectly honest—it must rank as one of the worst in the history of the club.

It will do no good to dwell upon it, let it be sufficient to say that it almost certainly doomed the club to seeking re-election.

My sympathy goes out to the Board. They took over at a most difficult time, when, to my mind, the club had been " running down " for a considerable period. They brought enthusiasm, a go-ahead spirit and the willingness to take a chance—and what has happened ? They have been let down on the field.

Even while I was writing these notes, a countrywide bid was being made to get the player or players to save the situation at the eleventh hour—or rather at a minute to midnight. Whether anything materialises or not, the effort has been made.

The team will have to get at least 14 points from the remaining games to have a chance of getting clear of the bottom two places. I would like to be optimistic, but there is nothing in the club's record this season which allows me to be so.

However, the unexpected has happened before to-day, and surely the team cannot possibly produce another performance like that at Oldham.

It is with the deepest regret we have to record the death last week of Mrs. H. McSteay, Secretary of the Barrow A.F.C. Development Branch. Our deepest sympathy is extended to Mr. McSteay and daughter. All local supporters of football will no doubt have appreciated her loyal assistance to the Barrow Club.

The away game at Barrow on 17 March 1956 saw a 2-1 win in a game that saw the debut of Roy Martin. The programme is one of the rarest post-war away programmes with very few printed for the 6,074 crowd.

Goalkeeper Terry Adlington made his debut against Crewe Alexandra in January 1957 in his only appearance in the championship season. After a spell with Torquay, he joined the new North American Soccer League with Baltimore Bays and later Dallas Tornado.

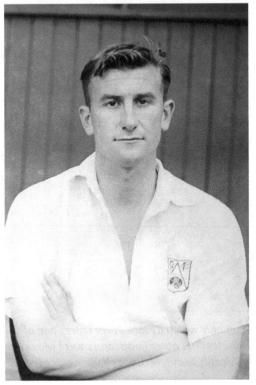

Ray Straw jointly (with Jack Bowers) holds the record for the number of league goals scored in one season – 37 in the promotion year of 1956-57 from Division Three (North). He made his debut in 1951 in Division One and eventually played in all six divisions after moving to Coventry and Mansfield.

The Osmaston End crowd basking in the sunshine at the beginning of September ahead of the match against Darlington. Alf Ackerman scored in a 1-1 draw in front of nearly 20,000 fans.

Tom Fairley in the Carlisle United goal can only watch as Jack Parry scores one of Derby's three second-half goals in 13 minutes. The other goalscorers were Mays and Ryan. Team: Webster, Barrowcliffe, Martin, Mays, McDonnell, Davies, Cresswell, Parry, Straw, Ryan, Powell.

Derby County Football Club Ltd.

Floodlit Football Match

Baseball Ground - Derby

Wednesday, 9th October, 1957

KICK-OFF 7 p.m.

DERBY COUNTY

versus

KILMARNOCK

Official Programme

3ᵈ·

As part of a regular number of friendly matches against Scottish opposition both at home and away, Kilmarnock provided the opposition in October 1957, both games finishing in draws, 1-1 at Derby and 2-2 in Scotland. These friendly games took place in October with the season in full swing.

1956-57. Division Three (North) Champions. Back: Storer (manager), McDonnell, Mays, Oliver, Webster, Martin, Davies, Young, Hann (trainer). Front: Parry, Powell, Brown, Straw, Ryan, Woodhead, Crowshaw.

The programme around Christmas time sported a special 'Seasons Greetings' cover that showed a snow-covered Baseball Ground. This one is for the fixture against Fulham on 21 December 1957, which ended as an entertaining 3-3 draw.

19 October 1957. Liverpool goalkeeper Younger is helped from the field suffering from an injury to his sciatic nerve which temporarily paralysed him. In these days, before substitutes, he returned to hobble around as a forward whilst Ronnie Moran went in goal. Derby won the game 2-1 with goals from Darwin and Woodhead.

21,304 fans turned up on 15 February 1958 to see this battle against fellow strugglers Notts County, a game Derby won 2-1, with Ryan and Woodhead scoring. Ken Oxford and Frank Upton are seen here in the middle of the action.

Harry Storer (centre) brought in Johnny Hannigan (left) and Dave Cargill (right) at the end of the 1957-58 season to bolster forward options. Hannigan arrived from Sunderland and Cargill from Sheffield Wednesday.

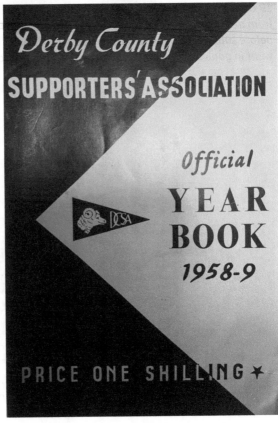

Derby County
SUPPORTERS' ASSOCIATION

Official
YEAR
BOOK
1958-9

PRICE ONE SHILLING ✦

The Derby County Supporters' Association produced a yearbook until the club began producing its own at the end of the 1960s. These yearbooks followed a similar format throughout the years, containing pen-pictures and profiles of the current playing staff, a team photo in the middle pages, fixture lists and various historical details.

1958-59 squad. Back: Hannigan, Mays, Daykin, Hann (trainer), Brown, Davies, Darwin. Middle: Hunt, Smith, Barrowcliffe, Oxford, Upton, Adlington, Martin, Powell, Young. Seated: Annable (secretary), Longson, Bates, Paul, Jackson (Chirman), King, Walters, Storer (manager). Front: Woodhead, Ryan, Womack, Parry, Clark, Bowers.

'It's a Goal!' was a card game produced by Pepys of Glasgow. Each of the 44 cards depicted a First or Second Division football club, Derby being the inside-right position from the 1950 set. These can be identified as being colour, full-length drawings and the reverse has a red back with cups and flags around a ball.
A second set was published in 1958 with a dull green back to the cards with a similar front.

DERBY COUNTY

FOOTBALL CLUB LIMITED

BASEBALL GROUND · DERBY

Phone 44850

DIRECTORS:

O. J. JACKSON, *President & Chairman*

C. R KING, C.B.E. *Vice-President*   F. B. WALTERS, *Vice-President*

F. O. BATES   H. PAYNE   W. H. PAUL   S. LONGSON

Manager : HARRY STORER   *Secretary :* C. ANNABLE

Official
Programme

2d.

Nk

PRACTICE MATCH

Reds v. Whites

Saturday, 16th August, 1958

Kick-off 7 p.m.

Printed by Derwent Press Ltd., Derby for Friary Publicity Ltd., Derby

The pre-season fixture was usually a match played between the first team and reserves, with the shirt colours being the name of the teams, in this case Reds v Whites. The programme, a four-page issue, is similar in style to that of a reserve-team programme issued at the time and it is interesting to note the kick-off time is 7pm on Saturday. Other similar matches in other years featured Whites v Blues.

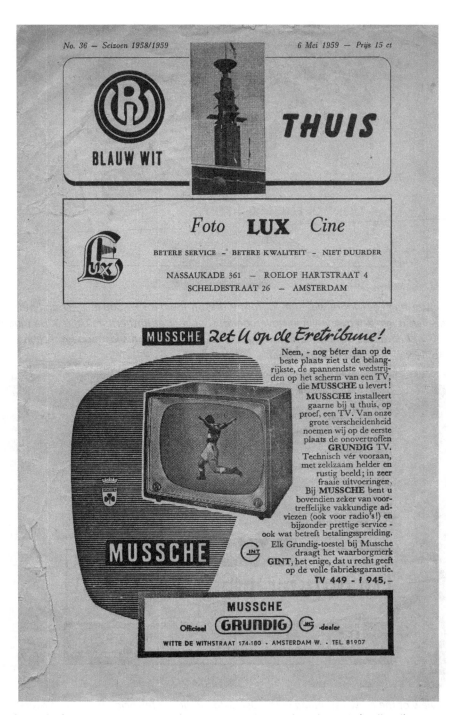
The end-of-season tour went to the Low Countries to play Blau Wit (Holland) on 6 May, winning 4-1, FC Red Boys (Luxemburg), winning 3-1, and Cercle Sportie Verviers (Belgium), winning 1-0. The rare programme from the first game is pictured.

Centre-half Les Moore was signed from Worksop Town for £1,000 in 1957 and made his debut in a 2-0 away win in November of that year at Rotherham United. He made 156 appearances during the following six and a half years, his last appearance in April 1964 was also at Rotherham.

A view of the crowd standing in the Osmaston Paddock terracing from the players' tunnel down to the 'C' Stand. We can see the edge of the pitch, only four feet from the crowd. In the distance there is a section of the 'C' Stand roof that has been deliberately cut out so those in the Osmaston Stand upper tier can see down into that corner.

DERBY COUNTY F.C. 1959-60

Left to right: (Back row) G. BARROWCLIFFE, A. MAYS, R. YOUNG, K. OXFORD, M. SMITH, A. CONWELL, F. UPTON; (Middle row) MR. H. STORER (Manager), R. SWALLOW, J. PARRY, J. HANNIGAN, G. DARWIN, P. THOMPSON, R. HANN (Trainer); (Front row) T. POWELL, G. DAVIES, D. CARGILL, G. BROWN

1959-60 squad. Back: Barrowcliffe, Mays, Young, Oxford, Smith, Conwell, Upton. Middle: Storer (manager), Daykin, Parry, Hannigan, Darwin, Thompson, Hann (trainer). Front: Powell, Davies, Cargill, Brown.

Ken Oxford, Ray Young and Frank Upton can only look on as the ball rolls towards the Derby net in this game against Huddersfield Town on 2 April. Two goals from Thompson and one from Hannigan gave Derby a 3-2 win.

DUNDEE United FC

Scottish League, Div. 2

Friendly Match

versus

Derby County

Tannadice Park

Saturday, 12th March

Kick-off 3 p.m.

(3d) *OFFICIAL PROGRAMME*

Derby were left with a blank Saturday due to Aston Villa playing Preston North End in the sixth round of the FA Cup. The Rams headed north and over the border for a friendly game against Dundee United on 12 March 1960, returning to play the rearranged match with Villa on 15 March. A crowd of 5,700 saw the hosts win 3-2, with Derby's goals coming from Thompson and Newbury.

This steam locomotive was built in 1936 and named 'Derby County'. It ran passenger services down the East Coast line into London until August 1959 when it was scrapped.

Originally numbered 2851, when British Rail took ownership of the train it was renumbered 61651. It was the fourth of 25 in a series of engines named after football clubs.

The only pieces to survive are the original nameplates which are in the hands of private collectors and worth over £35,000 each.

A limited edition of first day cover, postcard and print was produced by Dawn Covers in 1996. The Derby County locomotive is painted crossing the Friargate bridge.

Peter Taylor was the Middlesbrough goalkeeper and part of the managerial team that saw lots of success at Derby. Here he is seen making a rare save from an attack on a day to forget for the team that left them without a win so far in the season.

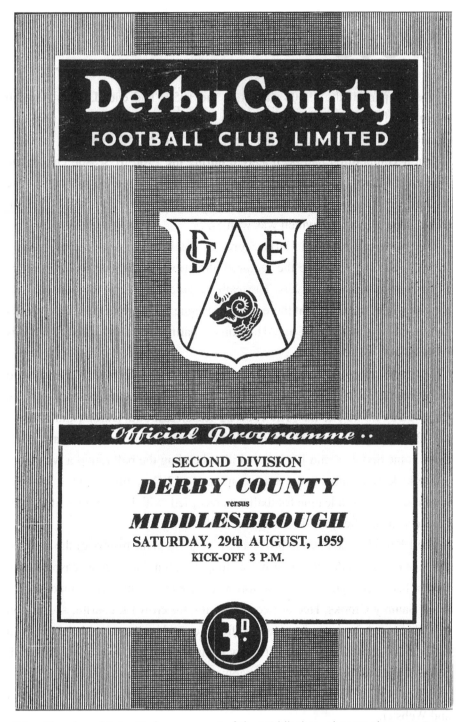

Brian Clough and Peter Taylor were part of the Middlesbrough team that won 7-1 at the Baseball Ground in August 1959. This was the biggest home defeat since Manchester City won by the same margin on 29 January 1938.

1960s

The early part of the 1960s started as the 1950s had ended, with the club averaging 15th place over the first four years of the decade. Bill Curry was signed from Brighton and was the top scorer for those four years.

A new competition had been started during the 1960-61 season called The Football League Cup, which at the time was not fully supported by many of the leading First Division teams, and Derby's first game in that competition was an away game at Watford, which was won 5-2.

Tim Ward had replaced Harry Storer as manager during the close season in 1962, but did not make the required alterations to the squad until injuries forced him to sign new players. The team struggled to survive that season, with the bad winter meaning that there were no league games for a number of weeks and they had to rely on a Curry-Hutchinson partnership that scored two thirds of the goals that season.

This lack of goals led to Ward signing Alan Durban from Cardiff City and Gordon Hughes from Newcastle United the following summer, and they were followed by Eddie Thomas. The 1964-65 season saw both Durban and Thomas net 22 league goals each in a season that saw Derby score more than any other team in the division, and Durban's skill at bending the ball round a wall from a free-kick was a most dangerous weapon. On 12 December 1964, one of the fastest-ever goals in league football was recorded, with Keith Smith of Crystal Palace scoring after just six seconds at Selhurst Park.

The 1966-67 season was to prove a turning point in the history of the club; on the face of the results not great in finishing 17th, but during that season Kevin Hector had been signed from Bradford Park Avenue on the recommendation of scout Sammy Crooks. Hector became an instant crowd favourite, scoring on his debut in a 4-3 win against Huddersfield Town. Tim Ward had taken the club as far as he could and a man with new ideas was sought, but to Ward's credit some of the players that were to become household names a few short years later had been brought to the club by him – Hector, Durban, Boulton, Daniel and Webster.

Brian Clough and his assistant Peter Taylor arrived from Hartlepool United and, despite finishing one place lower than the previous year, many new players

Ken Oxford had five years at Norwich City and played 128 league games before moving to Derby. During his five years at the Baseball Ground, Oxford made 162 appearances before moving to Doncaster Rovers.

Trade cards were just starting to appear in the UK, based on the US baseball and american football ones. These packs of cards also contained a stick of bubble gum, although it was often discarded. This packet is from the Anglo-American chewing gum co and these wax packets are very collectible, showing the club colours, badge and brief history.

had been brought in – O'Hare (Sunderland), McFarland (Tranmere), Hinton (Notts Forest), Robson (junior football), Barker (Burton) and Green (Rochdale) – a blend of young players and experience. As these new players were bought during the season, many of them were cup-tied for the League Cup and their replacements took Derby to their best-ever showing in the competition with a semi-final against Fist Division Leeds United.

During the following summer Clough somehow persuaded the legendary Tottenham Hotspur player Dave Mackay to join Derby and the jigsaw was completed when the experienced Willie Carlin joined early in the season from Sheffield United as well as John McGovern (Hartlepool) and Frank Wignall (Wolves). They went to the top of the table in late November 1968 and were to remain there. Along the way there were wins against First Division teams Chelsea and Everton in the League Cup, the former being hailed as one the great nights of football at the Baseball Ground as Derby came from a goal down to batter Chelsea, who eventually capitulated and let in three goals in the last 13 minutes.

Off the field, the first structural change to the Baseball Ground took place during the summer of 1969 when a new stand was built over the top of the Popside terrace, known as the Ley Stand (named after the factory behind that stand), and this brought the capacity up to over 41,000.

It did not take long to reach the maximum when 41,826 squeezed in on 20 September 1969 to see Tottenham Hotspur crushed 5-0 in the First Division.

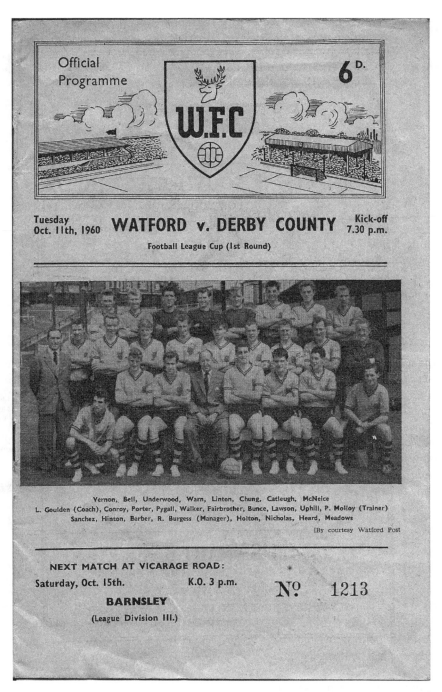

[By courtesy Watford Post]

The Football League Cup competition was introduced in the 1960-61 season, and in the first round Derby were drawn away at Watford. They came away with a 5-2 win with goals from Buxton, Hutchinson, Cargill, Hall and an own goal. Derby's team was Adlington, Barrowcliffe, Conwell, Young, Upton, Cargill, Swallow, Buxton, Hutchinson, Parry, Hall.

The squad wearing their new v-neck, short-sleeved shirts in 1961. Back: Barrowcliffe, Mays, Young, Oxford, Smith, Conwell. Middle- Storer, Swallow, Parry, Hannigan, Darwin, Thompson, Hann. Front- Powell, Davies, Cargill, Brown.

Frank Upton was a hard-tackling central-defender and played for Derby between 1954 and 1961 until he was sold to Chelsea, where he helped them secure promotion and also won a League Cup medal. He re-joined Derby in 1965 and played until September 1966, totalling 272 appearances.

Ray Young *first joined the Rams as a junior, before signing professionally at the age of 17 in 1951, making his debut three years later. He made the centre-half position his own for most of the following 11 years, making 268 appearances, one substitute appearance and scoring five goals.*

The match against Sunderland on 12 November 1960 drew the biggest home attendance of the season of 21,608. Barrie Hutchinson stabbed in a Curry header after just two minutes, although the visitors equalised before half-time.

Tommy Powell joined the club as a 16-year-old schoolboy during the World War Two. He made his debut in August 1948 and made 406 appearances for the club between 1948 and 1961, Derby being his only professional club. He is the father of Steve, who had a similarly long career at the club.

After announcing his retirement, Powell was presented with a Football League long-service award and a guard of honour greeted him before the league match with Ipswich Town in April 1961. He went along both teams shaking hands with the players, here with Frank Upton. He would have played in this game but was injured and played just three more games.

Former Coventry City, Chelsea and England goalkeeper Reg Matthews signed for Derby in October 1961. He is being watched by Chairman Harry Payne (left) and manager Harry Storer (right). He was to stay six years, making 246 appearances before being replaced by Les Green in 1968.

PLAYERS' AUTOGRAPHS, SEASON 1961/62 - DERBY COUNTY FOOTBALL CLUB.

T.ADLINGTON.	*(signature)*	T.POWELL.	*(signature)*
I.BUXTON.	*(signature)*	J.RICHMOND.	*(signature)*
G.BARROWCLIFFE.	*(signature)*	J.RICHARDSON.	*(signature)*
J.BOWLES.	*(signature)*	D.ROBY.	*(signature)*
J.CAMPION.	*(signature)*	R.SWALLOW.	*(signature)*
A.CONWELL.	*(signature)*	G.STEPHENSON.	*(signature)*
W.CURRY.	*(signature)*	P.THOMPSON.	*(signature)*
B.DAYKIN.	*(signature)*	P.WALLER.	*(signature)*
G.DAVIES.	*(signature)*	R.WEBSTE .	*(signature)*
M.HOPKINSON.	*(signature)*	M.WILLIAMSON.	*(signature)*
K.H.VINHAND.	*(signature)*	R.YOUNG.	*(signature)*
I.HALL.	*(signature)*	R.HANN(Head Trainer)	*(signature)*
B.HUTCHINSON.	*(signature)*	J.BOWERS(Asst.Trainer)	*(signature)*
L.MOORE.	*(signature)*		
R.MCANDREW.	*(signature)*		
R.MATTHEWS.	*(signature)*		
K.OXFORD.	*(signature)*		
D.PALMER.	*(signature)*		
J.PARRY.	*(signature)*		

The club would receive many requests for autographs throughout the season and so would produce pre-printed sheets that would be sent out. This one dates from the 1961-62 season.

Leyton Orient were the visitors on 20 January 1962, with The Rams lying in fourth place. Curry scored but was unable to stop a 1-2 defeat. Only two wins in the remaining 16 games saw them slip away to 16th place. Back: Barrowcliffe, Davies, Matthews, Parry, Hopkinson, Moore. Front: Roby, Havenhand, Curry, Swallow, Palmer.

Mike Cullen was a Scotland international inside-forward and was signed from Grimsby Town in November 1962 where he had made 178 appearances. He played in just 26 games, scoring five goals in his 21 months with the club. He moved on to <u>Wellington Town</u>*, where he played out his career.*

February 1962. Sam Ramsden, owner of the Trocadero Dance Hall (formerly the Alex cinema), presents a new flag to the football club.

DERBY
COUNTY
FOOTBALL CLUB
LIMITED

ANGLO-FRENCH FRIENDSHIP CUP-1st LEG
DERBY COUNTY
versus
A. S. BITERROISE
WEDNESDAY, 11th APRIL, 1962
KICK-OFF 7.15 p.m.

OFFICIAL PROGRAMME

*The Anglo-French Friendship Cup was a competition between the French and English
Second Divisions, with a team playing one of their counterparts home and away.
Derby played AS Beziers on 11 April, winning the first game 1-0 with a goal from Bill
Curry. Team: Matthews, Barrowcliffe, Conwell, Webster, Moore, Hopkinson, Hall,
Havenhand, Curry, Parry, Roby. Attendance: 6,987.*

ALLEZ... BÉZIERS !

ÉDITION SPÉCIALE

Bulletin Officiel de l'A. S. B. Football

Siège Social : « LE CONTI », Allées Paul-Riquet -- Téléphone 28.26.85

« REGIE EXCLUSIVE » de la PUBLICITE : Agence HAVAS

29, Allées Paul-Riquet - BEZIERS Tél. : 28-27-19 et dans toutes les succursales.

RENCONTRE INTERNATIONALE

COUPE DE L'AMITIÉ
FRANCO-BRITANNIQUE

DERBY COUNTY
A. S. BÉZIERS

Samedi 12 Mai 1962

Stade de Sauclières à 21 h.

There are no records or match reports for the return game on 12 May, the final score being 2-1 in favour of the French team, and there is no record of the Derby scorer. The overall winner of the competition was the English League, winning by ten points to the French six points.

Bobby Ferguson joined Derby from Newcastle United in 1962 and made 129 appearances over the next three seasons before moving to Cardiff City. He was appointed to the Ipswich Town coaching staff in 1970 and became manager for five years when Sir Bobby Robson was appointed England manager.

Derby splashed out £12,000 to buy Bill Curry from Brighton. He was an old-style centre-forward and a favourite of the fans, making his debut in October 1960. He played 164 games over the next four years, scoring 76 goals.

Curry (right) looks on as a shot from the floored Derby player flies into the net on a wet and muddy Baseball Ground.

Tim Ward was signed from non-league Cheltenham in 1937, and by switching playing positions from left to right wing this brought him his two England caps. After 14 years on the playing staff he was sold to Barnsley and eventually became another former player to return as manager in 1962, and he was responsible for signing Alan Durban and Kevin Hector.

Ward (right) meets some of the players on his arrival at the end of June 1962. The players seen with him are (left to right) Ken Oxford, Bill Curry, Bob Stephenson and Ray Young.

Chelsea were the visitors to the Baseball Ground on 26 October 1962 and left with the points after a 3-1 win. The Derby team pictured before the game was – Back: Barrowcliffe, Parry, Oxford, Moore, Waller, Ferguson. Front: Roby, Stephenson, Curry, Buxton, Mccann.

Ken Oxford (left), Tim Ward (centre) and Reg Matthews (right) are re-united at the Baseball Ground during the 1980s.

Jack Parry came from a footballing family and he made his debut towards the end of the 1948-49 season, scoring on his debut. He scored 24 league goals in the 1955-56 season before injury made him miss the last 11 games. He returned as captain in the Second Division and was a regular starter until the mid-1960s and made 517 appearances (110 goals), with only Kevin Hector making more league appearances for the club.

Glyn Davies was a Welsh schoolboy international when he joined Derby in 1948 as a 17-year-old. It took him four years to break into the team and he made over 200 appearances in nine years before moving back to Swansea.

Barrie Hutchinson scoring in the 20th minute of the last match of the 1961-62 season against relegated Brighton and Hove Albion on 28 April. The result was a 2-0 to Derby, with John Bowers scoring the other goal, their first win in seven games. 18-year-old winger Mick Williamson made his debut, the first of just 14 appearances.

Derby's defence under pressure from Southampton in November 1962. Hutchinson scored twice, and together with an own goal saw Derby win 3-1, just their third in the first 17 games. Ken Oxford and Bobby Ferguson are pictured on the goal line ready to deal with the danger.

Gordon Hughes was a native of County Durham and had played for Newcastle United. In August 1963 Derby paid £10,000 for him. On his day he was one of the most dangerous wingers in this division – not particularly tall, but was fast and determined.

Soccer Star ran from 1952 until 19 June 1970, 936 weekly issues in total. The issue dated 28 December 1963 carried a squad picture. Back: Barrowcliffe, Swallow, Waller, Oxford, Young, Matthews, Curry, Ferguson. Front: Havenhand, Hutchinson, Cullen, Parry, McCann, Durban.

A fishing trawler, number GY154, was built in Middlesbrough and took the name Derby County. Her maiden voyage was on 13 September 1933. The admiralty bought the boat in 1939 and converted it into an anti-submarine vessel.

Post-war it was re-registered as a fishing boat and eventually scrapped in Belgium during February 1964. An unusual picture of GY154 out of the water.

The match with Bristol Rovers in September 1960 ended in a 1-1 draw. Fagan (extreme right) makes a lunge for a cross from Parry that has evaded the defence. Derby County team: Adlington, Barrowcliffe, Conwell, Parry, Young, Upton, Swallow, Powell, Hannigan, Buxton, Fagan.

The match referee timed Jim Fryatt's goal for Bradford Park Avenue against Tranmere Rovers in 1964 at four seconds, although most observers disagree with the timing. Derby attempted to re-create the goal to disprove it.

Ian Buxton was one of those players who combined playing football in the winter months with cricket during the summer. He played for The Rams between 1959 and 1967 and Derbyshire Cricket Club from 1959 to 1973.

Brian Clough was not happy that he was unavailable for part of the season and moved him on to Luton Town fairly quickly.

A & BC were one of the most famous names in football trade cards and remain highly collectable today. They began producing football cards in 1954. 1963-64 saw Geoff Barrowcliffe, Ray Young (pictured) and Jack Parry appear in the set.

Jack Robson, who played for the club between 1928 and 1932, was landlord of the Talbot Inn in Belper. In September 1964 he invited over 20 former players for a get-together. Amongst them were Harry Bedford, Sammy Crooks and George Thornewell.

Čtvrtek 13. května 1965

SLAVIA-DERBY COUNTY

Mezinárodní utkání v kopané

a dojezd páté etapy cyklistického Závodu míru Drážďany—Praha

Sobota 15. května 1965   16.30 hodin

II. liga kopané — skupina A — 8, jarní kolo

Slavia - Spartak Motorlet

Předzápas: dorostenecká liga — skup. B — 8. kolo

SLAVIA — TEPNA NÁCHOD

Začátek ve 14.45 hodin

Nezapomeňte! V neděli 23. května zajíždíme k ligovému utkání s LIAZEM do Jablonce. Vypravíme opět autokary. Zájemci, hlaste se v sekretariátu. Odjezd opět z nábřeží proti Štvanici.

The end-of-season tour saw the team head to Czechoslovakia to play three games. The first was against Banik Ostrava (10 May 1965), followed by Slavia Prague (13 May 1965, pictured) and Otcokovioe (15 May 1965). Derby lost the first game 0-1, won the second 2-1, and drew the last 2-2.

Having lost the first three games of the 1965-66 season, they took the lead against Cardiff City on 1 September. Some woeful defending saw the Welsh team score five goals in response. Bobby Ferguson (shirt number three) can be seen diving to handball away a certain goal.

Reg Matthews stands stationery in front of the goal line with the ball heading towards the net from the resulting penalty kick.

George Best takes on most of the Derby defence during the FA Cup match on 22 January 1966. 33,827 fans saw Manchester United run out comfortable winners by 5-2. Derby's consolation goals came from John Richardson and Frank Upton.

Phil Waller pictured with Frank Upton. Waller had joined as a junior in 1961 and made 115 appearances over the following six seasons. He was sold to Mansfield Town by Brian Clough in March 1968 as he began re-shaping the squad.

Alan Durban was signed from Cardiff City in the summer of 1963 and initially was a prolific goalscorer before becoming a more orthodox midfield player. He represented Wales on 27 occasions and in all he scored 112 goals in 403 appearances in over ten years with the Rams. He returned as assistant manager to Roy McFarland in 1993.

This squad at the beginning of the 1966-67 season, with Tim Ward as manager, already contained several members of the Division Two and Division One teams over the coming decade, including Peter Daniel, Colin Boulton, Alan Durban and Ron Webster.

The previous two seasons had seen friendly matches against foreign opposition, and the 1966-67 season was no different. Maccabi from Israel were the visitors on Friday 12 August. Derby were victorious 2-1.

SIR ROBERTSON KING, K.B.E. *President*

F. B. WALTERS *Vice-President*
S. LONGSON *Chairman*
Manager—TIM WARD

H. PAYNE *Vice-President*
S. C. BRADLEY K. C. TURNER
R. KIRKLAND
Secretary—C. ANNABLE

Season 1966-67

DERBY COUNTY
FOOTBALL
COUNTY
CLUB LTD

TEL 44850   BASEBALL   DERBY
GROUND

Official
Programme
3d.

Friendly Match

DERBY COUNTY
VERSUS
MACCABI F.C.

Friday, 12th August, 1966
KICK-OFF 7.30 p.m.

Printed by Derwent Press Ltd., for Friary Publicity Ltd., Derby

In September 1966, Tim Ward (left) and Sam Longson (right) watch Kevin Hector sign from Bradford Park Avenue for a club record of £40,000. His goalscoring is second only to Steve Bloomer and he has made more league appearances than anyone else.

Hector pictured before the home defeat to Birmingham City in November 1966. Hector scored his sixth goal in his first ten games. Team: Matthews, Richardson, Daniel, Webster, Saxton, Waller, Hughes, Hector, Buxton, Durban, Hodgson.

Colin Boulton is recovering at home a day after the draw with Cardiff City in February 1967 with a badly cut eye. Bobby Saxton took over in goal whilst Boulton was off the field receiving treatment. He recovered in time to play in the next league game against Millwall.

The team for the last home game of the 1965-66 season against Preston, unusually wearing an all-white kit. Back: Webster, Waller, Saxton, Matthews, Upton (sub), Daniel, Richardson, Hodgson. Front: Hughes, Thomas, Buxton, Durban (the only goalscorer).

England's victory in the World Cup Final at Wembley Stadium in 1966 was marked by the Football Association by producing replica trophies, although not in solid gold. One was presented to each league club. Derby's can be seen in the cabinet in Main Reception at the stadium.

Derby County

Football Club Ltd.

YEAR
BOOK

Incorporating the activities of

DERBY COUNTY SUPPORTERS' ASSOCIATION

DERBY COUNTY DEVELOPMENT ASSOCIATION

1964 — 65

price sixpence

The annual yearbook followed the same format as previous editions, with pen pictures of the players, team photo, fixture lists and articles from the heads of the Supporters' Association.

The last game of 1966 was against Bolton Wanderers, with the team still in the lower reaches of the division. Phil Waller and Ian Buxton scored the goals in a 2-2 draw. Pictured left to right are Buxton, Durban and Hector about to head for goal after losing his marker.

Two days after Tim Ward was sacked in May 1967, the team to play Plymouth Argyle was picked by the directors. Pictured – Back row: Richardson, Daniel, Boulton, Saxton, Webster, Waller; front: Hughes, Draper, Thomas, Metcalfe (his only first-team appearance), Durban.

DERBY

COUNTY

FOOTBALL CLUB LIMITED

FRIENDLY MATCH

DERBY COUNTY
versus
HEART OF MIDLOTHIAN

MONDAY, 8th MAY, 1967
Kick-off 7.30 p.m.

OFFICIAL PROGRAMME — SIXPENCE

Derby entertained Heart of Midlothian on 8 May 1967 as part of their tour. A 1-1 draw followed in front of 5,000 fans. The following day Hearts played at Lincoln City before heading to Iceland.

Following the Hearts game, the players set off for their own tour of Germany. They played at Leipzig (17 May, won 2-1), Karl Marx Stadt (19 May, won 2-1) and Halle (22 May, drew 0-0). Clough and Taylor had been appointed before the departure – the party can be seen outside the team hotel in Leipzig.

Ron Webster, pictured on 1967, made his debut in 1962 having joined the club as an amateur in 1958. It was Brian Clough who converted him to a full-back during the 1967-68 season, a position he made his own for many years to come.

Alan Durban receiving a Wales international cap from chairman Sam Longson. He was a regular member of the Wales team, playing in 26 out of the next 30 games after his debut against Brazil in a World Cup warm-up game in 1966.

Part of the pitch was cleared for an inspection. In the days before under-soil heating, frozen pitches, snow and mud were no excuses to postpone a game. This view is taken from the back of the 'B' Stand looking towards the Normanton End.

18 July 1967, Brian Clough and Peter Taylor are meeting the players for the first time. Many of these players would be sold during the coming two seasons as the squad was re-shaped.

Brian Clough and chairman Sam Longson in conversation having met the players for the first time, many of whom would not last the season.

Happy to sit in the background, Clough's assistant (and former teammate at Middlesbrough) was Peter Taylor and he arrived with him from Hartlepools United. He had previously managed at non-league Burton Albion.

John O'Hare was Clough's first signing from Sunderland, where Clough has coached him in their youth team. His ability to hold the ball and create space for others was pivotal to the team and recognised by the manager who took him with him to Leeds United and Notts Forest.

Bobby Saxton played over 100 games in his three years before being one of the casualties of Clough's clear out of the established players to make way for different types of players more suited to his style. He was the first Derby substitute, replacing Barrowcliffe in a defeat to Southampton in August 1965.

Roy McFarland is welcomed to the Baseball Ground on 28 August 1967 following his £24,000 transfer from Tranmere Rovers. He was to play that night in a 3-1 win at Rotherham United. He has been captain, assistant manager and manager and is still at the club today as a director and club ambassador.

A very early Brian Clough squad from 1967. Back: Pat Wright, John Richardson, Peter Daniel, Reg Matthews, Bobby Saxton, Ron Webster, Colin Boulton, Roy McFarland, Phil Waller, Mick Hopkinson. Front: Gordon Hughes, Alan Durban, Kevin Hector, John O'Hare, Richie Barker, Alan Hinton.

John O'Hare scores on his debut, two minutes into the second half against Charlton Athletic in a 3-2 win on the opening day of the season. Webster (centre) and Hector (left) are pictured having lost their markers. Team: Matthews, Daniel, Hopkinson, Webster, Saxton, Waller, Hughes, Durban, O'Hare, Hector, Hodgson.

DERBY COUNTY
FOOTBALL CLUB
LIMITED

PUBLIC PRACTICE MATCH

DERBY COUNTY

VERSUS

NOTTINGHAM FOREST

SATURDAY, 12th AUGUST, 1967

KICK-OFF 7.30 P.M.

official programme — sixpence

The first time Derby fans would see a Brian Clough team at home was a pre-season friendly game against the previous year's First Division runners-up, Notts Forest, the visitors winning 1-3. Kevin Hector was on target for the Rams. Unusually, it was a 7:30pm kick-off on Saturday 12 August.

DERBY COUNTY
FOOTBALL CLUB
LIMITED

FOOTBALL LEAGUE CUP—2nd ROUND

DERBY COUNTY

VERSUS

HARTLEPOOLS UNITED

WEDNESDAY, 13th SEPTEMBER, 1967
KICK-OFF 7.30 P.M.

official programme—sixpence

As sometimes happens in cup draws, the first round of the League Cup competition saw Clough's former club Hartlepools United drawn against his new club. Derby triumphed 4-0 with goals from Hodgson and a hat-trick from O'Hare.

After four wins and two defeats in the league, Plymouth Argyle were the visitors and Derby had to settle for an own goal to win the game. Derby players can be seen clearing an Argyle attack – (left to right) John Richardson, Bobby Saxton, Peter Daniel, Roy McFarland, and Ron Webster.

Derby's 3-5 defeat at Bolton at the end of October 1967 was the start of a run of seven games without a win. Playing in their blue change kit, Saxton, McFarland, Matthews, Daniel, Webster and Durban clear another attack.

A 1960s cheer leader in front of the Osmaston End. From the picture, the crowd is still a predominately male audience. The small metal fencing went around three sides of the pitch, before being replaced by more substantial railings in the 1970s.

This team earned a creditable 1-1 draw at top-of-the-table Blackpool in December 1967, with John O'Hare scoring his eighth league goal of the season. Back: Saxton, Webster, Matthews, McFarland, Stewart, Richardson, Waller (sub). Front: Hughes, Barker, O'Hare, Durban, Hector.

Official Programme

LINCOLN CITY
FOOTBALL CLUB
Versus

Derby County

WEDNESDAY 8th NOVEMBER 1967

Fourth Round Replay

Kick-off 7-30 p.m.

Next Home Game

City v. Rochdale

WEDNESDAY 15th NOVEMBER 1967

Football League Division Four

Having beaten Hartlepool and Birmingham City, Derby were paired with Lincoln City in the next round of the League Cup. A well-deserved draw from the lower-league team meant a replay at Sincil Bank on 15 November 1967. A ground-record attendance of 23,196 saw Derby win 3-0 and progress to the quarter-final to play Darlington.

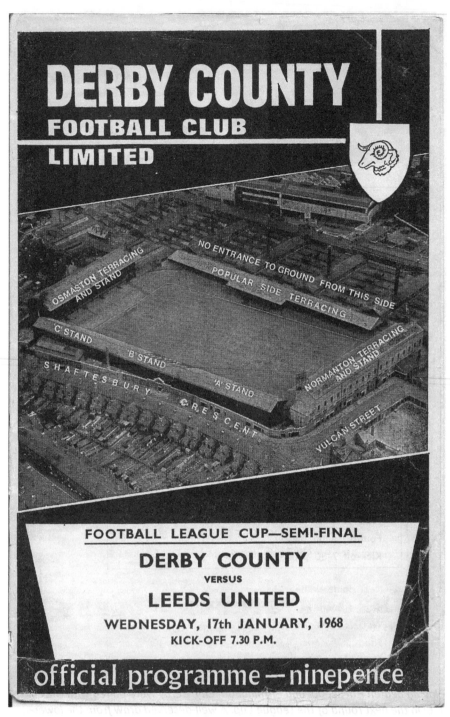

DERBY COUNTY

FOOTBALL CLUB

LIMITED

OSMASTON TERRACING AND STAND

NO ENTRANCE TO GROUND FROM THIS SIDE

POPULAR SIDE TERRACING

'C' STAND

'B' STAND

SHAFTESBURY CRESCENT

'A' STAND

NORMANTON TERRACING AND STAND

VULCAN STREET

FOOTBALL LEAGUE CUP—SEMI-FINAL

DERBY COUNTY

VERSUS

LEEDS UNITED

WEDNESDAY, 17th JANUARY, 1968

KICK-OFF 7.30 P.M.

official programme — ninepence

Having beaten Darlington 5-4, the draw for the semi-final wasn't kind to Derby, pulling First Division giants Leeds United out of the hat. The other teams involved in the semi-finals were Arsenal and Huddersfield Town.

Derby were coping well with their First Division opponents until an error by Bobby Saxton, who handled the ball in the penalty area. Johnny Giles scored the resulting penalty kick (pictured), despite Reg Matthews diving the right way. After this error, Saxton's time at Derby was short lived and he was sold to Plymouth.

The second leg of the semi-final saw Derby give a good account of themselves but they lost on the night 3-2 (4-2 on aggregate), with goals from Stewart and Hector. A week later, the two teams met again in the third round of the FA Cup. Leeds were once again victorious by 2-0.

Football League Review

the Official Journal of *The Football League*

PRESENTED BY COURTESY OF THE CLUB
VOLUME THREE Number 21 □ **ONE SHILLING**

The Football League Review, a free magazine included with the programme (issue 21), shows five-year old Claire Warrington of Littleover with her newly acquired ram, Fred. Fred originated from Bury, where a man wrote to the club and the Derby Evening Telegraph ran a story resulting in local business man Gordon Warrington acquiring it to go with a pony and horses in his fields. Claire said he likes to eat bran, grass, chocolate biscuits and cake.

The clock that was attached to the middle of the Osmaston Stand at the Baseball Ground was erected in 1968 as a gift from Sam Longson. The diameter of the face is 3½ feet and is encased in a wooden box with a perspex front. The clock has now been re-installed at Pride Park.

Derby's official club shop and promotions office was located at 55 Osmaston Road. This provided a place just out of the city centre where supporters could purchase the scarves, photographs, tankards, rammy banks, badges and other memorabilia. This is the official opening by management, directors and players.

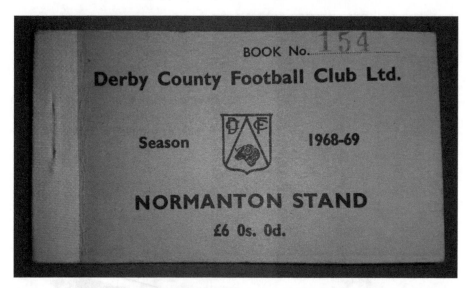

BOOK No. 154

Derby County Football Club Ltd.

Season 1968-69

NORMANTON STAND

£6 0s. 0d.

A season ticket for the Normanton Stand cost £6 in 1968 and contained vouchers that would be torn out as indicated on the boards hanging outside. They also allowed free entry to reserve matches and included the first four cup games as well.

The annual photo took place on 3 August 1968 with Dave Mackay absent. Back: Wright, Bostock, Webster, Boulton, Green, Rhodes, Butlin, Walker. Middle: Durban, Stewart, Barker, O'Hare, Hector, Hinton. Front: Richardson, Daniel, Robson.

The regimental mascot of the Mercian Regiment, known as Private Derby, is a regular visitor to the club for matches. Players Green, Webster, Boulton, Richardson and Durban can be seen with him.

The board of directors also had their picture taken with Private Derby: F. B. Walters, Stuart Crooks, Sir Robertson King, Sydney Bradley, H. Payne, K. C. Turner CBE, R. Kirkland, S. Longson (standing).

The signing of Tottenham Hotspur star Dave Mackay was a major coup for the club and a change of position to sweeper meant he could organise and direct players without doing the hard running he had to do previously. Here he is signing autographs on his arrival.

The Clough and Taylor team at the start of the 1968-69 season. It was not until Willie Carlin joined the squad after four games that results improved and they only lost twice with him in the team. Back: Arthur Stewart, John Robson, Les Green, Roy McFarland, Ron Webster, Dave Mackay. Front: John O'Hare, Kevin Hector, Richie Barker, Jim Walker, Alan Hinton.

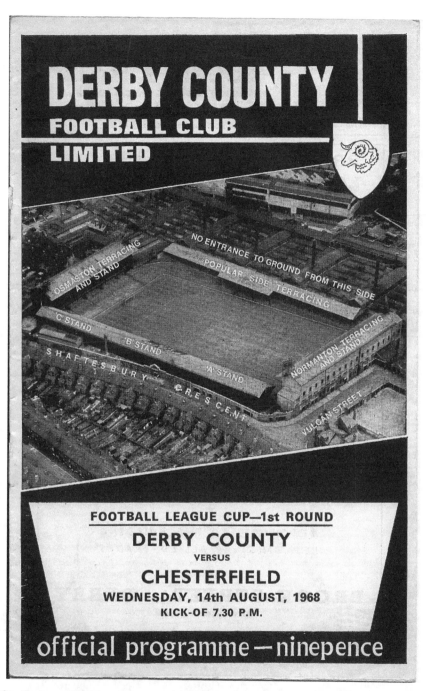

DERBY COUNTY
FOOTBALL CLUB
LIMITED

OSMASTON TERRACING AND STAND

NO ENTRANCE TO GROUND FROM THIS SIDE

POPULAR SIDE TERRACING

'C' STAND

'B' STAND

SHAFTESBURY

'A' STAND

NORMANTON TERRACING AND STAND

CRESCENT

VULCAN STREET

FOOTBALL LEAGUE CUP—1st ROUND

DERBY COUNTY
VERSUS
CHESTERFIELD
WEDNESDAY, 14th AUGUST, 1968
KICK-OF 7.30 P.M.

official programme — ninepence

After their semi-final appearance the previous year, the first-round draw put together an all-Derbyshire tie against Chesterfield. Goals from Hector, Hinton and an own goal saw Derby comfortably through. This was Les Green's and Dave Mackay's home debut. Team: Green, Richardson, Robson, Stewart, McFarland, Mackay, Walker, Barker, O'Hare, Hector, Hinton.

103

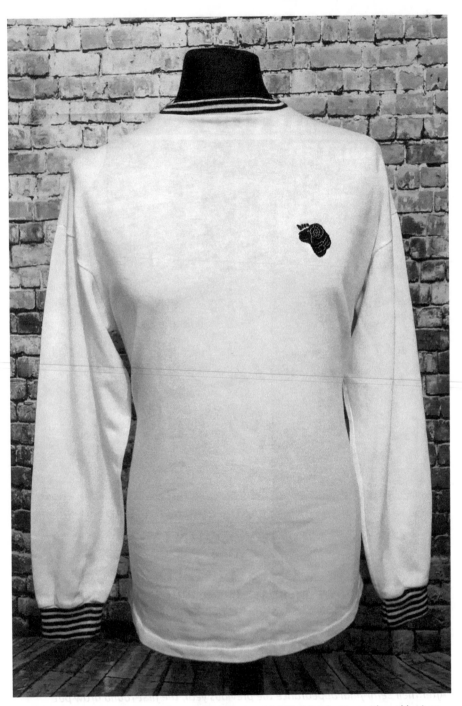

There was a new shirt design for 1968 with the shield badge being replaced by just the black rams head. The shirts, still white, changed from a 'V' neck at the start of the decade, ending with a round neck with black rings around it and the cuffs. Picture credit Phil Lowe.

After a slow start to the season (no league win in the first four games), Clough turned to Sheffield United's Willie Carlin for £60,000. The combative Liverpudlian midfielder was to provide the drive and tenacity in that area of the field, which was missing so far.

Chelsea
FOOTBALL CLUB

Wednesday, 25th September (7.30 p.m.)

CHELSEA
v
DERBY COUNTY

Football League Cup — Third Round

OFFICIAL
PROGRAMME

1/-

SEASON
1968-69

After beating Chesterfield and Stockport County at home, the third round saw a different prospect by being drawn to play Chelsea at Stamford Bridge. A confidence boosting 0-0 saw the Londoners have to face a replay in front of a packed Baseball Ground.

A long queue of fans wait patiently in the rain to get their tickets for the League Cup replay game against Chelsea in October 1968. 34,346 fans were to witness a landmark match.

The match ball from the Chelsea game, restored by collector Phil Lowe and formerly the property of Jim Walker who had kept it after the game.

Derby County

Jim Walker

Utility-forward

Jim Walker made his debut for *the Rams* against Blackpool on the last day of last season. He was signed from the Cheshire League club Northwich Victoria the previous Autumn. A clever ball player.

Football Club Ltd.

Baseball Ground Derby

LEAGUE CUP—3rd ROUND REPLAY

DERBY COUNTY

VERSUS

CHELSEA

WEDNESDAY, 2nd OCTOBER, 1968

KICK-OFF 7.30 p.m.

This game is commonly marked as the time when the fans began to see and believe that this was a team capable of playing at the top level. Goals from Hector, Durban and Mackay in front of the noisy fans under the lights with the smell of Ley's factory saw a famous 3-1 win.

D.C.F.C. LTD.

Derby County

v.

Everton

23rd Oct. 1968

Colombo St. Terracing

Admission 5/—

1027

Retain this Portion

Following a 0-0 at Goodison Park, fans again had to queue for their tickets, some going via the office and others through turnstiles, with the queue going behind the Osmaston End. The houses and buildings on Shaftesbury Street were to be replaced by the Shaftesbury Sports Centre.

A ticket stub for the Everton League Cup match. It was five shillings (25p) for a place on the Colombo Street terracing.

John McGovern was someone who Clough and Taylor knew well, having been his manager at Hartlepools United. He is pictured before his debut on 9 November in a 2-1 win against Charlton Athletic. His slight build and awkward running style made him an easy target for fans, but he was to develop into a skilled, two-footed midfield player.

Since McFarland signed from Tranmere he had been staying at the Midland Hotel next to the railway station. Dave Mackay moved in there when he joined the club as well. McFarland is seen here relaxing on the putting green in the garden of the hotel.

McFarland leaning on his Ford Capri outside the Midland Hotel.

Alan Hinton learnt his trade at Wolverhampton Wanderers where he earnt his England caps. Derby bought him from Notts Forest in 1967 as the squad was being re-built. He initially struggled to settle, but once he did his goalscoring and skill from a dead ball situation was unmatched in the league.

The Baseball Ground had remained unchanged since the building of the Osmaston and Normanton Ends back in the 1930s. Floodlights had been added on scaffolding poles in the 1950s and plans were in place to redevelop the Popside if promotion looked possible or likely.

After his sending off at Burnley in the FA Cup, John Robson had to attend an FA disciplinary hearing. Here he arrives with manager Brian Clough at the Midland Hotel. No further action was taken and he continued to play in all 42 league games.

The month of February, apart from one game against Cardiff City on the 1st, was written off, with every game postponed. Bob Smith, the groundsman, looks down the snow-covered field on the 13th with no prospect of it clearing.

ATHERSTONE TOWN
Association Football Club Ltd.

(Est. 1887)

Affiliated to the Birmingham County F.A.

Members of the West Midlands (Regional) League

Champions   1947-48   Winners
Birmingham Combination   Birmingham Senior Cup

Registered Office and Ground : SHEEPY ROAD, ATHERSTONE
Tel. Ath. 2760

President : S. DOWNS, Esq.
Chairman of Directors : H. L. BROADHURST, Esq.

Directors : Messrs. St. J. BROADHURST, H. S. HALL,
B. HOLLAND

Hon. Treasurer : St. J. BROADHURST, 72A, Queens Road,
Nuneaton.

Programme Editor and Match Secretary :
Miss. P. M. BROADHURST, 264, Lutterworth Road, Nuneaton.
Tel. Nuneaton 4822.

OFFICIAL MAGAZINE

SOUVENIR PROGRAMME

of the Visit of

DERBY COUNTY F.C.
Tuesday, 19th November

Derby played a pre-season friendly at Atherstone in 1967, and had arranged a mid-season game during the 1968-69 season, the game being played on 19 November.

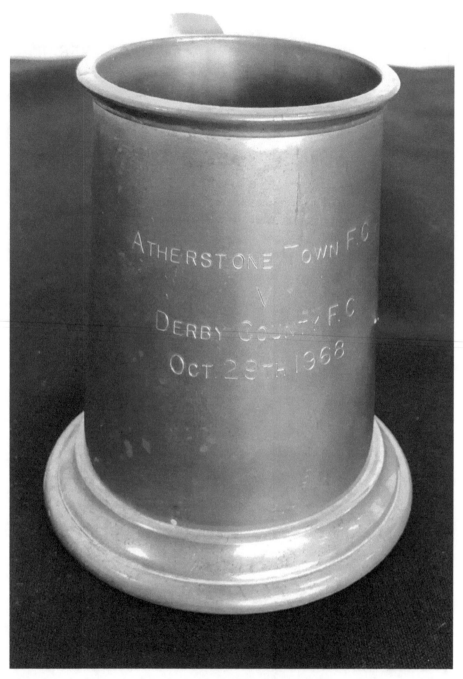

Players were presented with a tankard, engraved with the fixture details, dated 29 October. This original game had to be cancelled as Derby were to play Swindon Town on the 30th in the League Cup competition. Picture credit Phil Lowe.

GUERNSEY FOOTBALL ASSOCIATION

Guernsey

v.

Derby County

on

TUESDAY, 25th FEBRUARY, 1969

Kick-off: 5.0 p.m.

✦

PRICE · · · · · · 3d.

Whilst February's league matches were ruled out by bad weather, they kept themselves fit by playing several friendly games – Wycombe Wanderers, Stoke City and this one against Guernsey.

Goalmouth action from the away game with Blackpool as Les Green is slow to come out to a free kick in the 12th minute and is beaten by Brown to open the scoring. Derby hit back to win 3-2.

Les Green is watched by defenders Dave Mackay, Roy McFarland and John Robson in 1969. The old Popside terracing can be seen in the background with Offilers Ales painted on the roof. The same wording was also painted on the B Stand roof.

Pat Wright had made over 200 league appearances as a full-back for Shrewsbury Town before signing for Derby in 1967. He made 13 appearances in his first season but then spent two years in the reserves, unable to force past Robson and Webster, before moving on.

Frank Wignall had a very good scoring record in his career at Everton, Wolverhampton Wanderers and Notts Forest and had represented England. His signing boosted the forward-line options and covered for injuries. He made 38 starts and 18 substitute appearances, scoring 17 goals.

Derby's first goal against Bolton Wanderers on 5 April 1969 came from a long Les Green kick that Kevin Hector ran on to and lobbed over the on-rushing goalkeeper, Eddie Hopkinson.

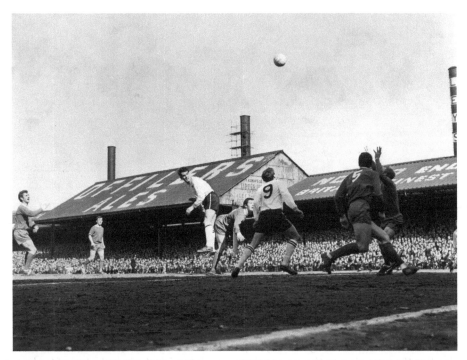

Wignall heads towards goal against Bolton as John O'Hare looks on. Two goals in four minutes from O'Hare and Carlin and others by Hector, Wignall and a McFarland goal on his 21st birthday made it a day to celebrate.

John O'Hare scores the third goal from a Hector pass against Bolton Wanderers in a 5-1 win and secured promotion in front of 30,684. This result was part of a run of nine successive wins. Team: Green, Webster, Robson, Durban, McFarland, Mackay, Wignall, Carlin, Hector, O'Hare, Hinton.

Celebrations in the dressing room after promotion was secured, with captain Mackay leading the way. Next to the glasses there is a plate of pork pie and a box of lard – not something the modern football coach would approve of.

A guard of honour is made by the Millwall players as Dave Mackay leads out the Rams on 12 April. A mix-up in the shirts meant that Derby had to play in the Millwall red away shirts.

A Willie Carlin goal gave the visitors a 1-0 win to continue the winning run and seal the championship. Green, Webster, Robson, Durban, McFarland, Mackay, McGovern, Carlin, O'Hare, Hector, Hinton. Attendance: 12,975.

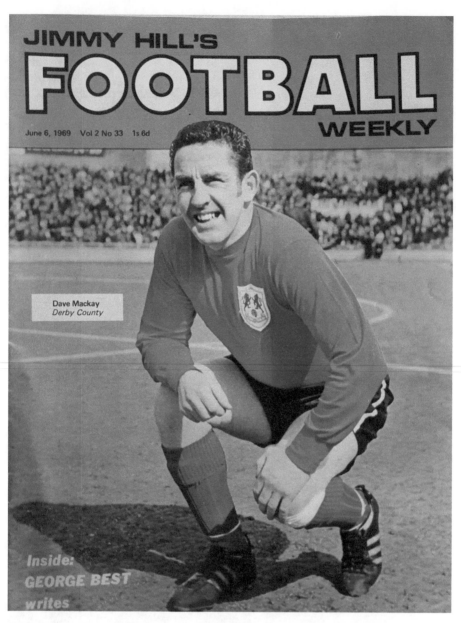

JIMMY HILL'S
FOOTBALL
WEEKLY

June 6, 1969   Vol 2 No 33   1s 6d

Dave Mackay
Derby County

Inside:
GEORGE BEST
writes

With the national press widely in attendance for pictures of the Division Two
potential champions, it was unfortunate that this was the day there was a kit mix-
up, meaning all the pictures from the day show them in the red shirts and socks
of the Millwall away kit. Here are two examples, the cover of Jimmy Hill's Football
Weekly magazine and (opposite), a photograph from Soccer Star.

Brian Clough taking part in a training session at the Municipal Sports Ground, with Frank Wignall looking on.

Before the last match of the season against Bristol City, the team were presented with the Division Two trophy and paraded it around the pitch for the fans. The championship was won by seven points from Crystal Palace and a massive 13 ahead of third-placed Charlton Athletic, losing only five league matches during the season.

DERBY COUNTY
FOOTBALL CLUB LIMITED

SOUVENIR programme 1s 0d
DERBY COUNTY versus BRISTOL CITY
Saturday 19th. April 1969

As the club comfortably won promotion to Division One, the last match of the season saw a special souvenir issue of the matchday programme produced that had an extra card cover around the normal match issue. The special issue shows the Division Two trophy on the front cover and individual player pictures on the back, together with their printed autographs. The cost of this special issue had increased to one shilling.

Waving to the crowds at the Osmaston End.

Dave Mackay holds aloft the Division Two trophy ahead of the final match of the season in front of the Popside.

The 5-0 result against Bristol City was as one-sided as it suggests, but it could have been worse had Alan Hinton not missed this penalty kick – more luck than judgement on the goalkeeper's part as it hit him and bounced to safety.

Les Green receives his medal in the directors' box after the final whistle, watched by Brian Clough (left) Afterwards, it was a party across the town, with Irongate Tavern having to close its doors at 9:30pm due to the large number of supporters. The players themselves were celebrating at the Midland Hotel where various speeches were given by the directors, 'a 45-minute epic' by the manager and one from the captain.

Brian Clough shakes hands with his captain Dave Mackay, holding the Division Two trophy. Peter Taylor, extreme left, looks on.

The 19 April, match edition for the Bristol City game was a 'Rams Souvenir Special' with many pictures of the matches throughout the season as well as a preview of the last match against Bristol City.

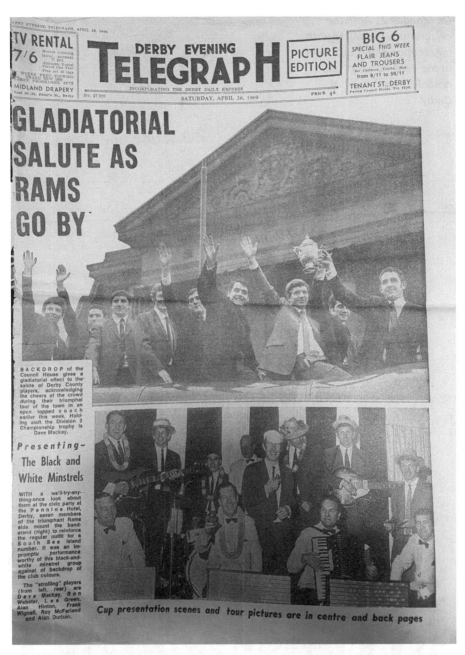

DERBY EVENING TELEGRAPH, APRIL 26, 1969

TV RENTAL
7/6
Weekly including
India, payment
If alamages Rental
Period One Year
Free set of jugs
WEEKS FREE VIEWING
THREE PROGRAMME SETS
MIDLAND DRAPERY
East St., St. Peter's St., Derby

DERBY EVENING
TELEGRAPH
INCORPORATING THE DERBY DAILY EXPRESS
No. 27,320
SATURDAY, APRIL 26, 1969
PRICE 4d.

PICTURE
EDITION

BIG 6
SPECIAL THIS WEEK
FLAIR JEANS
AND TROUSERS
for Children, Youths, Men
from 8/11 to 59/11

TENANT ST., DERBY
Faster Council House, Tel. 4141

GLADIATORIAL SALUTE AS RAMS GO BY

BACKDROP of the Council House gives a gladiatorial effect to the salute of Derby County players, acknowledging the cheers of the crowd during their triumphal tour of the town in an open topped coach earlier this week. Holding aloft the Division 2 Championship trophy is Dave Mackay.

Presenting—
The Black and White Minstrels

WITH a we'll-try-anything-once look about them at the civic party at the Pennine Hotel, Derby, seven members of the triumphant Rams side mount the bandstand (right) to reinforce the regular outfit for a South Sea Island number. It was an impromptu performance worthy of this black-and-white minstrel group against of backdrop of the club colours.

The "strolling" players (from left, rear) are Dave Mackay, Ron Webster, Les Green, Alan Hinton, Frank Wignall, Roy McFarland and Alan Durban.

Cup presentation scenes and tour pictures are in centre and back pages

One week after the last match, another 'Picture Edition' of the paper shows the team in front of the Council House on their open-top tour of the town and has the headline 'Gladiatorial Salute as Rams go by'.

On Monday 21 April the celebrations continued with a Reception and Dance held at the Pennine Hotel and hosted by the Mayor of Derby.

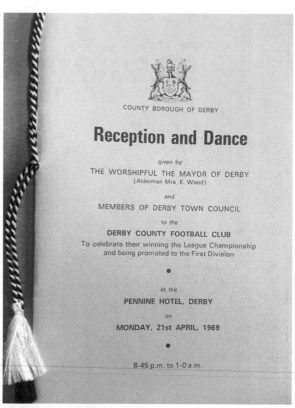

COUNTY BOROUGH OF DERBY

Reception and Dance

given by

THE WORSHIPFUL THE MAYOR OF DERBY
(Alderman Mrs. E. Wood)

and

MEMBERS OF DERBY TOWN COUNCIL

to the

DERBY COUNTY FOOTBALL CLUB

To celebrate their winning the League Championship
and being promoted to the First Division

•

at the

PENNINE HOTEL, DERBY

on

MONDAY, 21st APRIL, 1969

•

8-45 p.m. to 1-0 a.m.

Dave Mackay and Frank Wignall lead the team to the reception in their honour.

The crowds surround the Council House as the team and mayor appear on the steps.

A police horse and other members of the constabulary hold back the crowds.

Inside the Council House, Dave Mackay takes a drink from the trophy, held by Miss Derby County, Pat Wheeldon. Miss Wheeldon had already won the Miss Britain title and went on to become Miss Western Europe.

Some of the players join the band, with Mackay and McFarland on guitar, Les Green on drums and Alan Hinton leading the singing.

Sam Longson takes the trophy to show some of his staff in his office at Chapel-en-le-Frith.

Back: Peter Taylor, Wignall, Robson, Webster, Green, McFarland, Durban, Mackay, Clough. Front: Walker, McGovern, O'Hare, Carlin, Hector, Hinton.

Directors:
S. Longson,
Clough
(manager),
Sir Robertson
King KBE
(president),
K. C. Turner CBE
(vice chairman),
S. C. Bradley
(chairman),
R. Kirkland,
F. B. Walters
(vice president),
H. Payne
(vice president).

On Wednesday the victory tour went from Derby up the A6 to Matlock for a reception at the County Offices. Sandwiched between the two receptions was a friendly at Nuneaton Borough and there were still two more testimonials to play during the week at Notts County (Alex Gibson) and Coventry City (Brian Hill).

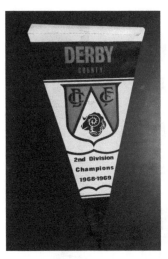

Another collectable came in the form of pennants, generally triangular printed plastic with a hanger cord. These usually carried the club logo and were often issued to commemorate a trophy or event.

A more common version with a club logo together with '2nd Division Champions 1968-69'.

Another popular collectible from this era was enamel badges. Original ones are quite valuable compared to the plethora of modern soft enamel variants we see on sale today.

The limited-edition collectors plate was made for the 20th anniversary of winning the Division Two trophy and are individually numbered on the reverse. Drawings of 13 players and management surround the plate, which is finished with a gold rim.

Les Green was one of the shortest goalkeepers in the Football League. He was signed from Rochdale but had previously played for Peter Taylor at Burton Albion and then followed him to Hartlepools United to team up with Clough. He was ever-present in the 1968-69 and 1969-70 seasons.

Mackay added to his huge collection of medals and personal accolades by being awarded the Footballer of the Year. For this season it was uniquely split with Tony Book of Manchester City for their efforts in guiding their respective clubs to trophies, and Mackay himself had played in 52 out of the 54 matches, more than he had ever done.

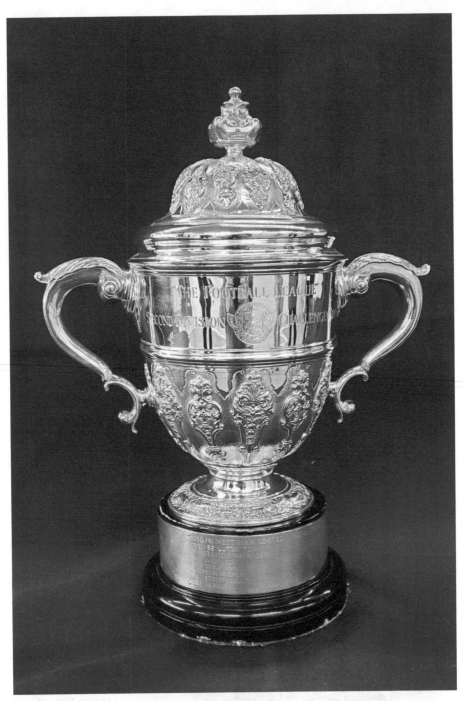

The Division Two trophy was introduced in 1958. The base is engraved with the club that won it, and on close inspection it is engraved with Derby winning it in 1986-87, yet it was never officially presented to them as the league was sponsored by the Today newspaper who had their own trophy.

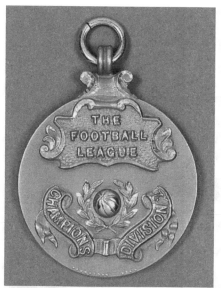

A Division Two winners' gold medal, as presented to Dave Mackay, which the club now own. They were presented with blank backs, allowing the player or club to have them engraved with their name, if required. A limited edition of 100 of these replicas was produced to commemorate the 50th anniversary during the 2018-19 season.

Derby County Community Trust and Quad hosted an evening with some of the players from the 1968-69 squad to mark the 50th anniversary. Left to right: Colin Gibson and Roger Davies (hosts), Alan Hinton, Roy McFarland, Alan Durban, John O'Hare and Jim Walker.

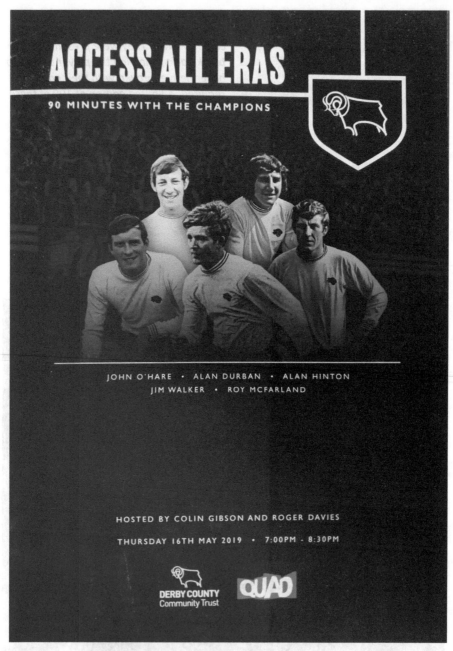

A special event programme was produced for the '90 minutes with the champions' event that listed all the league results and other items of interest.

DERBY COUNTY FOOTBALL CLUB LTD.

BRIAN CLOUGH (Manager)
MALCOLM BRAMLEY (Secretary)

Telegraphic Address: "FOOTBALL DERBY"
Telephone: DERBY 44850

BASEBALL GROUND · DERBY
DE3 8NB

Dear Season Ticket Holder,

Now that we have reached the end of another season, I would like to take this opportunity of giving you some idea of our hopes and plans for the future.

It goes without saying that without the enthusiastic support you have given us during the past season it would have been impossible to progress as far as we have. It is no secret that you made it possible to spend £100,000 on new players and neither is it a secret that the efforts to strengthen the side could mean the spending of a further £100,000 during the close season.

I mentioned the word 'progress' because we feel it has been tremendous but as far as points and the position in the League are concerned, you must be as bitterly disappointed as I am. However, you know (together with many other people, judging by the number of new applications received for tickets) that we are on the verge of providing a successful Derby County team.

I have enclosed a copy of the new season ticket prices and I am sure you will agree that with all the increased expenses, together with what is to be spent on new players, they are justifiable.

Included in our future plans is a drastic improvement in the refreshment facilities for our season ticket holders and at the risk of getting my knuckles rapped by my Board of Directors, I have no hesitation in saying that at present they leave a lot to be desired.

Finally, on behalf of my Board of Directors I want to thank you for the magnificent support you gave us last season because without your continuing support, no progress could be made at all.

Yours sincerely,

BRIAN CLOUGH, *Manager.*

Brian Clough personally signed thousands of letters to season-ticket holders. The new Ley Stand was to be opened before the first First Division home fixture against Burnley – fans were encouraged to buy two years in advance

Sidney Bradley owned a menswear clothing shop on East Street, Derby, selling ready-made suits and accessories. He joined the board in December 1960 and was chairman at the time when club were promoted from the Second Division in 1969 and was vice-chairman throughout the early 1970s.

Setting off on a pre-season training run at Nottingham Racecourse. The squad is led by Gordon Guthrie and Jeff Bourne. Also in the leading group is Dave Mackay, with Butlin, Boulton, Durban, Webster, Hector and Hinton at the rear.

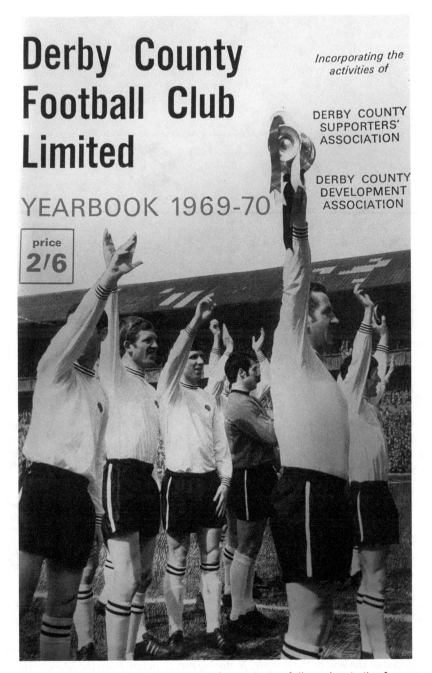

Derby County Football Club Limited

YEARBOOK 1969-70

price
2/6

Incorporating the activities of

DERBY COUNTY
SUPPORTERS'
ASSOCIATION

DERBY COUNTY
DEVELOPMENT
ASSOCIATION

The yearbooks produced by the Supporters' Association followed a similar format throughout the years containing pen-pictures and profiles of the current playing staff, a team photo in the middle pages, fixture lists and various historical details. The 1969-70 one has a picture on the cover instead of the usual black and white, and an attempt has been made to colourise it by adding green for the grass and on the facia on the stand.

One of the first jigsaws to be produced with a Derby subject was a 240-piece puzzle produced at the end of the decade, featuring match action from the Manchester United home game of 1969-70. The picture shows Roy McFarland's back and Brian Kidd against a background of the main ABC Stand at the Baseball Ground. This puzzle came in a plain brown box, simply labelled 'Derby County 240-piece jigsaw puzzle'.

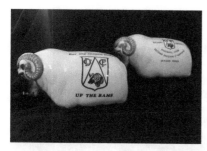

The Rammy banks were introduced in the late 1960s and were a ceramic money box in the shape of a ram. Some of these just had the club logo on the side, whilst others had slogans such as 'For my season ticket'. These were produced regularly for a number of years and completing a full set of these is quite a task. As these were produced for children and not as ornaments, one would expect that many of these have been damaged or broken and thrown away since then.

An unusual item on sale was a tray, which had the club badge and printed signatures of the players

Ceramic tankards had been on sale at the Supporters' Shop (soon to be renamed The Ramtique), but there was a special edition made in 1969. Picture credit Phil Lowe.

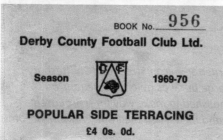

A season ticket for the Popular Side Terracing for the first season back in the First Division cost £4 for all league games, Central League games (reserves) and the first four cup matches. The 1969-70 season also marked the opening of the new £150,000 Ley Stand and priority would be given to those who would purchase a two-year ticket, the cost being £25 for both seasons whereas a single season 'B' Stand ticket cost £12 and 10 shillings.

Derby travelled to Fortuna Koln on 27 July for the first pre-season game, with other fixtures to follow against Wacker Biberach and MVV Mastricht before returning home.

FORTUNA-KURIER

OFFIZIELLES ORGAN DES SC FORTUNA KÖLN · 26. Juli 1969

FC Derby County — stehend von links nach rechts: Frank Wignall, Alan Durban, Les Green, Ron Webster, John Robson, Roy McFarland, Jim Walker — sitzend von links nach rechts: John McGovern, Willie Carlin, Dave Mackay (Kapitän), Kevin Hector, John O'Hare, Alan Hinton

The Baseball Hotel was situated on the corner of Vulcan Street and Shaftesbury Crescent, opposite the football club. The large bar was able to serve fans on their way to the game. The hotel was demolished to make way for a proposed redevelopment of the ground that was abandoned when the Pride Park site became available.

The first home game and first chance to see the new Ley Stand was against German team Werder Bremen on 5 August, resulting in a 6-0 win. The programme cover for the first few matches showed Les Green against an artist's impression of the new structure.

1969/70

R.B. BROOKS	*(signature)*	
C. BOULTON	*(signature)*	
P. DANIEL	*(signature)*	
A. DURBAN	*(signature)*	
L. GREEN	*(signature)*	
K. HECTOR	*(signature)*	
A. HINTON	*(signature)*	
D. MACKAY	*(signature)*	
R. McFARLAND	*(signature)*	
J. O'HARE	*(signature)*	
J. RICHARDSON	*(signature)*	
J. ROBSON	*(signature)*	
J.A. RHODES	*(signature)*	

A. STEWART	*(signature)*
R. WEBSTER	*(signature)*
J. WALKER	*(signature)*
W. CARLIN	*(signature)*
F. WIGNALL	*(signature)*
J. McGOVERN	*(signature)*
R. PATRICK	*(signature)*
T. KANE	*(signature)*
J. BOURNE	*(signature)*
R. MARLOWE	*(signature)*
A. LUDZIK	*(signature)*
P. WRIGHT	*(signature)*

The amount of exposure given to the club after promotion meant many more requests for autographs from fans up and down the country. Plain, copied sheets were available with the first team and reserves.

152

The first game of the season was at home to Burnley, the team that knocked them out of the FA Cup competition the previous year and reports at the time thought they were lucky to win and keep all their players on the field as they spent most of the time fouling the Derby players.

Derby could not find a way though the Burnley defence and had Les Green to thank for coming away with a 0-0 draw with this penalty save that he cleared with his legs. John Robson (number three) is looking on.

Alan Hinton putting pressure on the Burnley defence, with goalkeeper Peter Mellor missing this cross. John O'Hare, John McGovern and Ron Webster look on. Exterior cladding to the front of the Ley Stand had still not been fixed up.

The Municipal Sports Ground was used as a training ground. Willie Carlin (left), Kevin Hector (in action) and John Richardson (holding the ball). They are being marshalled by Jimmy Gordon.

Dave Mackay wanted to win every match, league or cup, and even in training as the floored player will testify to.

Roy McFarland made four England Under-23 appearances during the 1968-69 season and his continued development alongside Dave Mackay pushed him towards the full squad. He was named as a reserve for the Mexico World Cup squad.

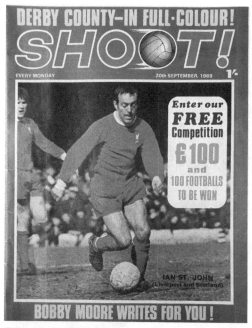

Shoot! magazine was a weekly publication that was launched a year after Goal and its first issue came out on 16 August 1969. Usually the middle pages contained a double page colour team picture. Derby featured in this issue, number six, on 20 September.

The first home win came in a mid-week game against Ipswich Town by a 3-1 scoreline, despite going behind to Ipswich's first goal of the season. Alan Hinton's penalty levelled the score before he scored again before half-time. Carlin added a third in the second half.

Ticket stub from the 'B' Stand for the match against Tottenham Hotspur on 20 September 1969 that attracted an unsurpassed attendance of 41,826.

Derby County Football Club Ltd.
SEASON 1969 — 1970

FIRST DIVISION

DERBY COUNTY

versus

TOTTENHAM H.

SATURDAY, 20th SEPTEMBER, 1969

Kick-off 3 p.m.

OFFICIAL PROGRAMME

1/-

A match programme from the game that saw Derby's record home attendance. This was one of six games during the 1969-70 season that attracted crowds of over 40,000. Because of the large numbers of programmes printed, it is not as valuable as one might think or hope, although it should be part of everyone's collection as it was an historic day for the club. This programme also included a leaflet from Bell's Whiskey congratulating Brian Clough on being named as Manager of the Month for August 1969.

John O'Hare has scored the fifth goal and is congratulated by Carlin, McGovern and Hector as they recorded their fifth successive victory.

Mackay enjoying himself against his former teammates. Derby are beating Dave Mackay's former team, Tottenham Hotspur. The final score was 5-0 to Derby with two goals from Alan Durban and one each from Willie Carlin, John O'Hare and Kevin Hector.

SHEFFIELD WEDNESDAY F.C.
OFFICIAL MAGAZINE

Hillsborough,
Saturday, September 27th 1969
Kick-off 3 pm

WEDNESDAY WORLD

Volume 1
Number 6

1/-

SHEFFIELD WEDNESDAY

(Royal blue shirts, white sleeves, white shorts)

1—PETER SPRINGETT
2—WILF SMITH
3—KEN BURTON
4—GERRY YOUNG
5—SAM ELLIS
6—TOMMY CRAIG
7—ARCHIE IRVINE
8—PETER EUSTACE
9—ALAN WARBOYS
10—DAVID FORD
11—GRAHAM PUGH
Sub.

DERBY COUNTY

(White shirts, black shorts)

1—LES GREEN
2—RON WEBSTER
3—JOHN ROBSON
4—ALAN DURBAN
5—ROY McFARLAND
6—DAVE MACKAY
7—JOHN McGOVERN
8—WILLIE CARLIN
9—JOHN O'HARE
10—KEVIN HECTOR
11—ALAN HINTON
Sub.—FRANK WIGNALL

Referee: V. J. Batty (Helsby Cheshire) Linesmen. Red flag: E. Jolly (Manchester). Yellow flag: J. Wrennall (Chorley Lancs).

After the first 11 matches of the season, Derby were top of the table after five successive defeats. The first defeat came at Hillsborough against Sheffield Wednesday. Over 44,000 packed the stadium, with huge numbers making the short journey from Derby. Just one goal against the run of play settled the game.

FOOTBALL MANAGERS AWARD
ENGLAND

This is to Certify that

Brian Clough

Manager of

Derby County Football Club

has been nominated by a
panel of Leading British Sportswriters as
THE FOOTBALL MANAGER OF THE MONTH

September, 1969

This certificate is awarded to the Football Manager whose club is a member of The
Football League or The Scottish Football League and who, in the opinion of the
judges, has personally given most to his club to help them fulfil their ambitions.

MANAGING DIRECTOR,
ARTHUR BELL & SONS LTD.
SCOTCH WHISKY DISTILLERS,
PERTH. SCOTLAND.

*Brian Clough was nominated as Manager of the Month for September 1969 for four
league wins in the month.*

Another 40,000-plus crowd greeted Manchester United on 4 October. It was a one-sided game where Derby's collaborative effort outshone the individual skills of the United stars. Les Green was in fine form.

Kevin Hector, hidden behind Willie Carlin, has just beaten the United defence at the near post to open the scoring. The ball nestles in the net with Dunne, Stepney and Fitzpatrick wondering how Hector beat all of them.

The ball is in the back of the United net again – this one disallowed despite McFarland and Durban pointing. The referee is already blowing for a foul and the linesman on the far side also has his flag raised.

Continued pressure brought a second goal with Fitzpatrick (centre) getting in the way of a cross and deflecting it past Stepney before John O'Hare could pounce.

One of the issues associated with 1970s football was the rise of hooliganism, typically identified by the skinhead and bovver boot. Pictured with Sgt George Johnson are confiscated boots from away fans in the tunnel during the game, to be collected afterwards.

FOOTBALL LEAGUE CUP COMPETITION
5th ROUND (Replay)

UNITED REVIEW

THE OFFICIAL PROGRAMME OF MANCHESTER UNITED FOOTBALL CLUB

no. 13

NINEPENCE

*Photo by the
Press Association*

MANCHESTER UNITED v. DERBY COUNTY
NOVEMBER 19th 1969   **KICK-OFF 7-45 P.M.**

Derby were to face United twice more before the turn of the year, in the League Cup fifth round. After a 0-0 draw at the Baseball Ground, they travelled to Old Trafford on 19 November, with United winning 1-0. A modern version of the programme cover was used for the League Cup game in the 2018-19 season.

The Liverpool fixture attracted 40,993 fans as Derby maintained their impressive start to the season. An astonishing 4-0 win meant they had beaten both Merseyside teams, Tottenham and Manchester United, scoring 13 goals and conceding just one. Scorers against Liverpool were McGovern, O'Hare and two from Hector.

Back Row (from left) JOHN ROBSON, ALAN DURBAN, ROY McFARLAND, LES GREEN, RITCHIE BARKER, DAVE MACKAY (Captain)
Front Row (from left) RON WEBSTER, WILLIE CARLIN, JIM WALKER, JOHN O'HARE, ALAN HINTON, KEVIN HECTOR

Photograph by courtesy of the Daily Express

Derby County Football Club

BASEBALL GROUND · DERBY · DE3 8NB
Telephone 44850 and 42374

October					NOVEMBER · 1969								December				
					SUN	MON	TUE	WED	THU	FRI	SAT						
Sun	-	5	12	19	26	-	-	-	-	-	-	1	Sun	-	7	14	21	28
Mon	-	6	13	20	27	2	3	4	5	6	7	8	Mon	1	8	15	22	29
Tue	-	7	14	21	28	9	10	11	12	13	14	15	Tue	2	9	16	23	30
Wed	1	8	15	22	29	16	17	18	19	20	21	22	Wed	3	10	17	24	31
Thu	2	9	16	23	30	23/30	24	25	26	27	28	29	Thu	4	11	18	25	-
Fri	3	10	17	24	31								Fri	5	12	19	26	-
Sat	4	11	18	25	-								Sat	6	13	20	27	-

Published by DERBY COUNTY SUPPORTERS' ASSOCIATION
55 Osmaston Road, Derby, DE1 2JH. Telephone 44522

This official club calendar for 1969 contains a colour photograph of the team taken in the early part of the 1968-69 season. The same image was used for an Esso poster that could be obtained from petrol stations.

In the 14th minute of the game against West Bromwich Albion, the Albion goal was peppered by shots from Wignall, Hector and Durban, whose shot ballooned out to O'Hare, eight yards out, who placed his header firmly into the corner of the net.

Another Wales international cap for Alan Durban, this time presented in the dressing room by the directors. Other full internationals were to represent the club shortly – McFarland and O'Hare at full international level and Robson at under-23 level.

The Park Drive book of Football ran for three years, produced by the cigarette company. It included a mixture of pictures (some colour), text and statistics covering the previous season's action.

As Park Drive continued to market to football audiences, they introduced plastic cigarette cases with a push out section that carried the club's logo. There seems to have been over 30 different teams' cases produced.

Roy McFarland and Dave Mackay sitting down for dinner at the Midland Hotel on 29 December, no doubt discussing tactics and future opponents.

The forerunner to the modern Merlin and Panini sticker collections in the UK was started by a company called FKS Publishing in 1967 and generally limited to the First Division players, 15 players per team and cost 6 pence for a packet of 7 stickers. They were not stickers as we know them today but coloured pictures that were to be stuck along one edge into an album. The earliest of these Derby 'stickers' was in the 1969 set, called 'The Wonderful World of Soccer Stars in Action' and it featured some lesser-known players from the Derby squad such as John Richardson and Arthur Stewart.

The Subbuteo football game had been invented in 1947, and the 1960s saw the production of the now legendary three-dimensional OO scale figures which continued until the manufacturers ceased. A number of generic kits were produced, with Derby falling under kit ten, plain white shirts and black shorts. All the teams themselves were hand-painted and assembled by a thriving cottage industry using the housewives of Tunbridge Wells.

A special Derby County version of the number-ten kit was available that had the added collar and cuff trim and stripe on the shorts. This set is very rare as named teams were not normally produced at this time and prices realised at auction are over £300.

Francis Lee, floored and nearest the camera, has just scored the winning goal from a breakaway despite the protests from Peter Daniel, standing in for Roy McFarland. In the background we see the old-style half-time scoreboard. Team: Green, Webster, Robson, Durban, Daniel, Mackay, McGovern, Carlin, O'Hare, Hector, Hinton. Sub: Wignall. Attendance: 40,788.

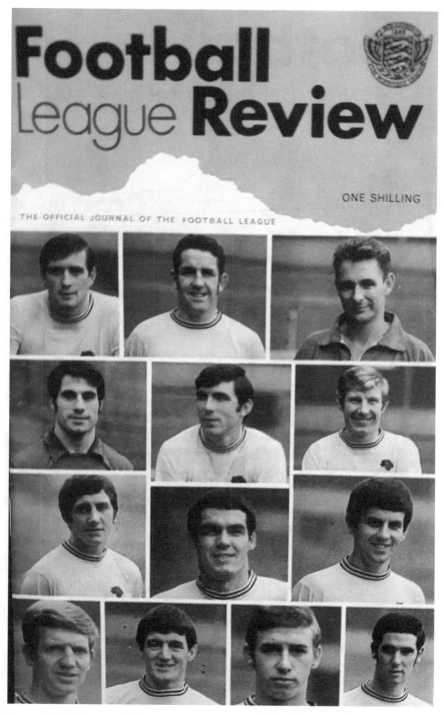

Football League Review

ONE SHILLING

THE OFFICIAL JOURNAL OF THE FOOTBALL LEAGUE

There were 366 issues of the magazine, written and printed by the Football League and included with matchday programmes. These are becoming very collectable items. Many people have a few of these but very few people have them all.

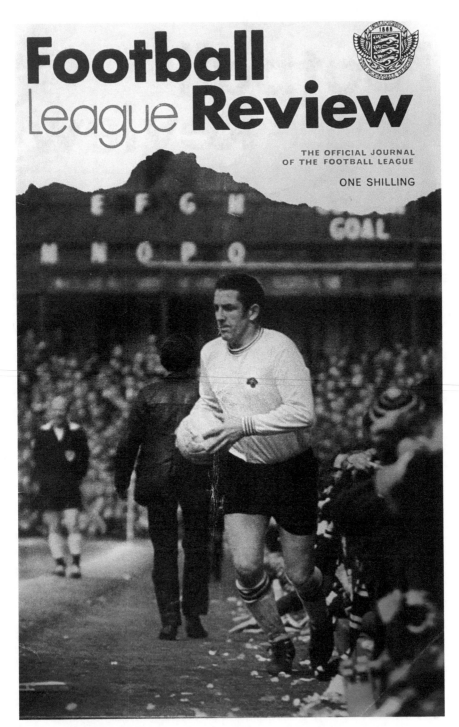

In all they printed and produced 100 million copies in just under ten years that involved 7,000 pages and two million words. Over 300 colour team photographs were printed in the issues.

Ian Storey-Moore beats Les Green to a cross in the game against Notts Forest on 29 November 1969, which the visitors won 0-2. Moore was paraded in front of the Derby fans thinking they had signed him in March 1972, but he had actually signed for Manchester United after Forest refused to sanction the deal. Two months later Derby were champions.

The players having a Christmas party at the York Hotel on 22 December, pulling crackers. From the front, left: Hector, Webster, Durban and Hinton. Right: Carlin, Robson, O'Hare and Green. At the end of the table is a smiling Peter Taylor.

World Sports magazine in December 1969 ran its lead article on Derby's return to the First Division and the background on the cover is made up of many newspaper headlines from the previous months.

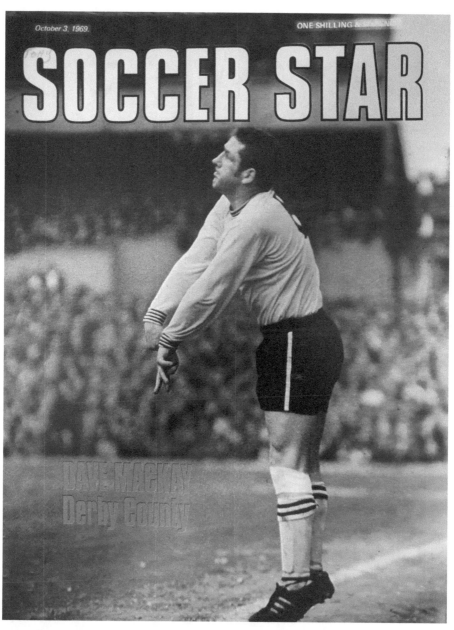

Dave Mackay was the focus for many of the football magazines and regularly featured on the cover, including Goal and Soccer Star.

The cover of Rover comic of 13 December shows a drawing of Kevin Hector's goal in the 2-2 draw at Chelsea.

Terry Hennessey, the Wales captain, signed from Notts Forest in February 1970 for a club-record transfer fee of £100,000. Here, signing a contract, he is carefully watched over by Clough and Taylor.

A brief walk out onto a frozen Baseball Ground.

Dave Mackay leads out the team for an away game.

That image was recreated as a statue by sculptor Andy Edwards and stands next to the Players' Entrance at Pride Park Stadium. It was unveiled in September 2015.

A first training session and meeting up with other influential members of the team – Mackay and McFarland. He made his debut on 11 February in a 2-2 draw with Chelsea.

Willie Carlin, Alan Hinton, Kevin Hector and John McGovern take part in a Shrovetide race with chefs on 10 February 1970.

The Baseball Ground pitch was a major problem when there was prolonged rain. In an attempt to try and resolve issues, various methods were tested on the drainage. What was known as 'the grave' was dug.

BV - #0001 - 151019 - C0 - 234/156/10 - PB - 9781780915937